"Rob Eagar views relationships throug[h] love and acceptance, bringing hope [and] lasting joy. *Dating with Pure Passion* [...] seeking God's design in lasting relationships."

Louie Giglio
founder of Passion Conferences

"Rob Eagar helps singles no longer feel like second-class citizens. *Dating with Pure Passion* points out how true fulfillment and great relationships are found by discovering pure passion for God and others."

Shannon Ethridge
bestselling author of the
Every Woman's Battle series

"*Dating with Pure Passion* communicates a message that singles of all ages desperately need to hear."

Scott Hitzel
Pastor to Singles, Saddleback Church

"Rob Eagar offers a rare blessing indeed: a male perspective on romance. *Dating with Pure Passion* is armed with insights, honesty, and truth to help singles forge healthy relationships with each other, with themselves, and with God."

Camerin Courtney
Managing Editor of
Today's Christian Woman

"With balance, depth, and deep honesty, Rob Eagar explores the heart of romance for singles and aspiring couples who are wondering if their relationship is truly one for keeps. *Dating with Pure Passion* is a must-read for anyone trying to navigate today's dating scene with integrity."

Paula Rinehart
bestselling author of
Sex and the Soul of a Woman

"Rob Eagar writes as if he is inside the heart and head of the reader. *Dating with Pure Passion* is a must for singles who hunger to experience life to the fullest. It skillfully depicts what passionate living looks like and shows how to get there. I heartily recommend it."

Dr. Steve McVey
bestselling author of Grace Walk

"Rob Eagar has an extraordinary ability to connect with single adults at the deepest level. He lovingly points singles to Christ as their source of wholeness and preparation for successful relationships."

Steve Grissom
President, DivorceCare

"*Dating with Pure Passion* is a must-read for all Christian singles that will be referenced and recommended for a lifetime. It is one of the precious few books that present hands-on teaching about our identity in Christ— the power to live out what the author proclaims. Rob has done this well."

Dr. Bill Gillham
bestselling author of
Lifetime Guarantee

"After many years of counseling Christian couples who relate out of emotional baggage and misconceptions, I'm thankful to see a book that helps single men and women understand that fulfillment and completeness can only be found in Christ."

Dr. Anne Trippe
marital and family therapist

"Too many Christian dating resources just resemble popular self-help therapies. *Dating with Pure Passion* gets it right by teaching singles about their completeness in Jesus Christ. Rob Eagar shows singles how the love of God can transform all facets of their lives, especially the way they date."

Scott Tanksley
Director of Single Adult Fellowships
North Point Community Church,
Atlanta, Georgia

"*Dating with Pure Passion* is more than just another how-to book on dating. Instead, Rob Eagar teaches truths of being a new creature in Christ and illustrates how these principles can manifest themselves appropriately in a Christian dating relationship."

Don Munton
Minister to Single Adults
First Baptist Church, Houston, Texas

"*Dating with Pure Passion* is an outstanding tool for singles! Rob Eagar will help you set healthy emotional and physical boundaries, attract the opposite sex, date for the right reasons, and enjoy completeness in Christ. I'd recommend it to any of my single friends!"

Holly Wagner
author of God Chicks *and*
When It Pours, He Reigns

DATING WITH PURE PASSION

ROB EAGAR

HARVEST HOUSE PUBLISHERS

EUGENE, OREGON

Cover by Terry Dugan Design, Minneapolis, Minnesota

Cover photo © Digital Vision

DATING WITH PURE PASSION
(Formerly published as *The Power of Passion.*)
Copyright © 2002 by Rob Eagar
Published by Harvest House Publishers
Eugene, Oregon 97402
www.harvesthousepublishers.com

Library of Congress Cataloging-in-Publication Data

Eagar, Rob, 1968–
    [Power of passion]
    Dating with pure passion / Rob Eagar.
        p. cm.
    Includes bibliographical references.
    ISBN-13: 978-0-7369-1670-7 (pbk.)
    ISBN-10: 0-7369-1670-9 (pbk.)
    1. Single people—Religious life. I. Title.
    BV4596.S5E24 2005
    248.8'4—dc22   2005001512

Printed in the United States of America

07 08 09 10 11 12 / VP-CF / 10 9 8 7 6 5 4

To my wife, Ashley,
whose unyielding reliance upon Jesus Christ
and commitment to our relationship
has made marriage more passionate
than I ever dreamed.

I love you.

Acknowledgments

No author can write a book without the assistance of others, and I want to thank those who helped make this project a reality:

To Barry Grecu and Richard Harris, who first encouraged me to follow the desires that Christ placed within my heart.

To my parents, Bob and Betsy Eagar, my sister, Melanie, and my in-laws, Joel and Judie Padgett, for supporting me when I quit my job to follow my dream.

To Andrea and James Fowler for donating a computer during the writing process.

To all of the focus group participants who contributed stories and insight to this book, including the Atwood and McMichael families, Nancy, Jan, Jim, Andrea B., Deane, Erika, Dave, Mona, Lisa, Dave, Charles, Dawn, Kevin, and Malissa.

To Lori Burton, Gray Absher, Anne Trippe, Bob Christopher, Greg Smith, Steve McVey, and Tom Grady for their patience to read and comment on my rough manuscripts.

To my agent, Greg Johnson, for your counsel and encouragement.

To everyone at Harvest House for supporting me and helping me spread my message of Christ's passion to the world.

To my wife—Ashley, you are the most beautiful and wonderful woman in the world. I will forever be thankful for your encouragement, advice, editing, and tireless sacrifice. You endured so much for the sake of "the book." Most of all, you believed in me when I almost gave up. Thank you for being my best friend. I am so madly in love with you.

To my Lord and Savior, Jesus Christ, who created me, rescued me, and loves me more than life itself. May my life and this book be a reflection of Your glorious, passionate love!

Contents

:: :: ::

1

THE POWER OF PURE PASSION

:: :: ::

Discovering the Longing of Your Heart

I don't ever want to see you again." Her words stung as I listened on the phone in disbelief. Around the room, pictures of her stared back at me. In one image, she smiled, wearing her favorite dress. Another photo captured her laughing on our first date. And nearby, a large portrait framed her as she beamed in her wedding gown.

"I love you. Please don't go," I begged. Instead, the phone went dead, and so did our marriage.

I huddled on the sofa in our new apartment. Only seven months earlier, we had joyfully joined as husband and wife. What happened? I thought she loved me. How could she discard our relationship so casually? *Surely, she will come back,* I thought.

A week later, my best friend visited to buoy me in my loneliness. "Why would she leave me?" I asked him. "I am devoted to her."

"Maybe there is hope if she is still wearing her wedding ring," he said.

Wanting him to be right, I walked into our bedroom, where her clothes and the scent of her perfume remained. I fumbled through her jewelry tin and prayed that I wouldn't see a small, sparkling stone....

But there it lay, the precious symbol of my commitment. It was true—my wife no longer loved me. I crumpled to the floor in shock as my friend rushed to catch me. In agony, my heart faltered, and my lungs fought for air. My whole body seemed to shut down as I sobbed uncontrollably. I would have died in tears had my friend not been with me that evening. Like a brother, he supported me and kept me from losing my mind.

My dream of lifelong intimacy crumbled before my eyes. "Is this it?" I cried. "Is this all you get after falling in love—a broken heart and your name added to the divorce statistics?" Emotions of despair, anger, and humiliation hit me all at once.

My life became a living hell when the woman I deeply loved deserted me. In the ensuing months, food lost its taste, and my body shed 18 pounds. At night I cried myself to sleep. In the morning my only solace was to stand in the shower until all of the hot water ran out. At work I was reduced to mindlessly staring at the wall. Nothing could relieve the immense ache within me.

The Longing for Love

Each of us is created with a heart that desperately needs love, and this need does not disappear as we get older. The longing only intensifies. Shields of innocence and hope preserve our hearts through much of the pain during childhood. But when we enter romantic relationships as adults, our exposure to the cruel realities of this world becomes unavoidable. Interacting with fellow singles, we discover that the love we crave can be elusive. Someone dumps us, another person disappoints us, or the opposite sex ignores us. Soon, we realize that love from other people cannot be guaranteed.

Thus, we carry a yearning inside for someone to approve of us, to cherish us, and celebrate that we exist. Even with success in our careers, hobbies, or church activities, we conclude that life is pointless without love. Deep down, we know fulfillment doesn't come from worldly accomplishments. Our hearts want something more—they want to flourish in the joy of an intimate relationship.

This desire is apparent as we each seek our "happily ever after." We dream of the perfect soul mate. We read romantic novels and cry when two lovers tenderly unite. We cheer in movies when the hero rescues his beauty. It is undeniable. We roam this planet in search of *passionate love*. And for most single adults, dating is considered the means to achieve this earnest goal.

The Great Dating Crusade

After seven months, the grief from my wife's abandonment began to subside. Healing occurred through my endless prayers and the reassurance of concerned friends and family. I will never forget how they rallied around me in my dark hours. They planned dinners, trips, and parties, all designed to distract me. They called me day and night to reaffirm their care for me. Through their warmth and attention, my heart began to recover, and a new optimism for romance developed.

At the age of 29, I wanted to prove to myself that I could secure a love that wouldn't leave me. I reasoned that my first marriage had failed simply because I had dated the wrong woman. If I made a better choice in the future, such as dating a more devout Christian, then surely I would experience a fulfilling relationship.

So with a heart hungry for love, I embarked on a Great Dating Crusade. For two years I scoured the metropolis of Atlanta, Georgia, in search of Miss Right. I visited every church group, singles Bible study, and dance social that I could locate. In addition, my buddies and I wandered the trendy singles bars, hoping to encounter a wise, Christian woman tucked away in some smoky corner.

Over time, my romantic campaign generated some results. I attracted the attention of a young woman at church who fascinated me with her beauty and godly reputation. My heart savored every moment with her as we shared extravagant dinners at the finest restaurants I could afford. Feeling high from rediscovering romance, I was convinced that our future had potential—until she chose to leave the country as a missionary. Her decision disappointed me, but I remained steadfast on my mission of love.

Several months later, my heart found relief in a pretty woman who initiated an interest in me. She flirted, planned fun activities, and quietly leaned on my arm as we walked around town. The sweet taste of her affection sent my self-esteem soaring and electrified my confidence. Victory in love seemed evident—until she stated her wish to see other guys. I chalked it up as another relationship that started off hot but abruptly crashed in frustration.

Determined to satisfy my longing for love, I pressed ahead into a third dating endeavor. This time, I was sure that my heart would be fulfilled. A vivacious woman had fallen for me, and I utterly adored her. At times, the chemistry between us exhilarated me. Within months, everyone considered us to be the perfect couple, and we started to meet each other's parents.

However, in the midst of our excitement, dissimilar ideas about God and issues about her family suddenly drove us apart. I ended our relationship but felt angry that another fruitless romance had resulted. *What does it take to find love in this world?* I silently brooded. I couldn't understand why intimacy seemed so evasive. No matter whom I met, love never lasted.

Practice for Divorce

I have a close friend who jokes that dating in our current society is practice for divorce. In many ways, he's right. The state of romance among Christians is disheartening. Examine marriage within the church, and you'll find that the divorce rate is as high as the world's. Observe how Christians date, and you'll find that virginity is out of style because so many women give their bodies to sex-hungry guys.

Yet the Bible says that faith in Jesus Christ is supposed to lead to a fulfilling life. If so, where is this life? Why is the hope of a satisfying romance or a lasting marriage so fleeting?

Consider your dating life. How many times have you thought, *Surely I have found my soul mate*, only to watch the relationship disintegrate and your heart remain empty? Is it difficult to meet other Christians worth dating? Do you wonder if you will ever find real love?

Wherever I go, I meet jaded, heartbroken, and defeated individuals. A bitter breakup, a one-night stand, or an unwise decision scarred their hearts. With disappointed or hardened attitudes, they seem resigned that a good relationship is beyond their reach.

I meet other singles whose hearts are exhausted under the weight of dating do's and don'ts. They are taught to strap on legalistic principles and live by them. Yet this burden to obey rules restricts their ability to be themselves or develop intimacy with another person.

Shouldn't Christians be the ones who understand real love? If so, then why are mature dating relationships so scarce within the church? Why do half of the Christian singles who get married wind up divorced? Why are so many single men and women giving up their pursuit of true love?

Gorging on Chocolate Love

Have you ever gone a long time without eating and felt your stomach groan with hunger? In those situations, what was your body telling you? Obviously, it was crying out for some nutritious food. Yet, how often have you consumed chocolate out of desperation or convenience just to get rid of those hunger pangs? I've done it several times. What happens?

Initially, feeding your empty stomach with chocolate feels great. The ache goes away, your hunger disappears, and all of the sugar and caffeine hitting your system gives you the sensation of feeling "high." Buzzing with bliss, you wonder why you don't eat chocolate for breakfast, lunch, and dinner.

About 30 minutes later, however, everything changes. A sharper pain than the one before grips your stomach, and your head becomes dizzy. All of your pleasant feelings degenerate into discomfort worse than your original hunger.

What caused this pain to result? Was there something wrong with the chocolate? No. Chocolate is safe to eat, but it doesn't contain the nutrients necessary for your body to survive. Therefore, when you are hungry, chocolate alone cannot help you. Instead, it makes you feel worse. For your body to thrive, it must receive a steady diet of nutritious food. Then you can enjoy chocolate as a fun dessert. However, you will get sick if you try to live solely on chocolate.

Unfortunately, eating chocolate on an empty stomach illustrates how a lot of singles build dating relationships. They approach one another with hungry hearts, hoping that the other person will feed them. This condition can be especially acute when a man or woman feels lonely, rejected, or starved for acceptance. Without love, people become desperate for something to fill the void inside their hearts. A romance, with its potentially sweet taste and emotional highs, seems the likely solution to their hunger.

Consider my Great Dating Crusade. I was hungry for love and searched repeatedly to find a woman to fulfill me. Every new romance that I entered felt like a chocolate sugar high with soaring emotions, exhilarating self-esteem boosts, and a sweet sense of security. In the headiness of romantic rapture, my heart thought that a woman could fulfill me forever. Nevertheless, the euphoria inevitably collapsed. Sometimes it took weeks. Other times, it took months. My wife's happiness vanished after a year of dating and seven months of marriage.

Regardless of how wonderful a new dating relationship feels, the romantic bliss will eventually wear off. Human affection may taste good, but like chocolate, it cannot give our hearts what they need for survival. *The true hunger of our hearts is to be accepted unconditionally.* We need more than just attention, friendship, or sex. We long for someone to love us despite our faults, mistakes, and imperfections. Our hearts remain hollow when no one completely accepts us.

Humans, however, cannot give each other unconditional love. We get upset or impatient when someone fails to make us happy. Furthermore, we base our love for someone on how well they perform. The root of this problem is *sin*, which causes constant mistakes, conflicts, and disappointments. No one is accepting, patient, and forgiving all of the time. Therefore, human love is like chocolate because the pleasure doesn't last. None of us have the ability to accept people unconditionally. The affection we give to each other may taste good initially, but the thrill disappears as our selfish motives demand performance. And this problem lasts from the cradle to the grave.

For instance, when you were younger, how often were you scorned for having acne, wearing braces, fumbling the football, or failing to meet your parents' expectations? As a single adult, how much pressure do you feel to wear the right clothes, appear rich and successful, or socialize with the popular crowd? Looking ahead, how frequently do you see elderly people neglected because they think too slowly, can no longer drive, or pose a financial burden to their families?

I don't mean to sound fatalistic, but we must acknowledge the reality that human love is performance-based. It always has been and always will be. You can date anyone in this world, but that person cannot give your heart the unconditional acceptance that it craves.

This truth also applies in marriage. Someone once asked a pastor, "What is your wife's opinion of you?"

He replied, "It depends on what day you ask her. Some days she loves me. Other days, I drive her crazy, and she wonders why she married me. My wife and I wish we could love each other perfectly, but it is impossible since we both sin and make choices that hurt each other. God is the only Person who loves us regardless of how we act."

As Christians, many of us believe that romantic passion will fulfill us. We pray for God to send us a soul mate, and then we date one person after another, trying to get him or her to love us. Our relationships start off well, but then rejection or disappointments tear them apart. Meanwhile, those singles who get married report that marriage isn't what they thought it would be.

Consider those around you. How many of your married friends warn you that marriage is tougher than you think? Yet, how many of your single friends complain of feeling incomplete without a spouse?

All too often, we neglect what our hearts really need and attempt to satisfy ourselves with a cheap substitute called *romance*. In essence, we try to live on the relational equivalent of chocolate. But our hearts cannot survive under the demands of performance-based love. We inevitably burn out, wear out, or drop out from trying to please others.

In my case, I had to reach total exasperation before I grasped that dating and marriage would never fulfill me. I appeared successful to many people because I'd had several girlfriends and reached my goal of marriage. Those romances, however, never fulfilled me. Either I required too much of a woman or she expected too much of me. We were sincere in our desire for lasting love, but we couldn't make it happen.

Some within the church advise that our hearts would be fulfilled if we simply changed our dating methods. They advocate going back to courtship, going online, reinstituting arranged marriages, or embracing a new set of dating guidelines. Yet they overlook the truth that no matter what style of dating you adopt, you still wind up dating a person whose love for you is tied to your performance.

Therefore, this book is not about subscribing to a new set of dating principles or techniques. It is an offer to pursue what your heart truly wants. A perfect love waits to delight you. This love, however, cannot soothe the ache within your heart until you stop chasing after romantic passion or passionate sex. Those shallow quests lead to emptiness. The hunger in your heart is for *pure passion.*

Jesus replied, "I am the bread of life. *No one who comes to me will ever be hungry again*" (John 6:35 NLT).

What Is Pure Passion?

How can you know for sure that another person loves you? Can you be certain based on what he or she says? No, "I love you" doesn't mean much these days. Countless couples say it while dating, but then they break up. What about a person who makes a formal commitment? Can you rest assured that their love will last? Sadly, promises of love rarely endure. If they did, divorce wouldn't be so common.

According to the Bible, you know that someone loves you when that person chooses to die for you. First John 3:16 (NIV) says, "This is how we know what love is: Jesus Christ laid down His life for us." When Jesus innocently died on the cross, He left no doubt that He was deeply in love with you.

This truth was great news for my hungry heart. I realized that Christ's death was a declaration of proof that He loved me. But I continued to wonder, *If Jesus is holy, and I still sin, then how could He love me despite my mistakes? Isn't His love performance-based just like everyone else's?*

> But when the kindness of God our Savior and His love for mankind appeared, *He saved us, not on the basis of deeds* which we have done in righteousness, *but according to His mercy*, by the washing of regeneration and renewing by the Holy Spirit, whom He poured out upon us richly through Jesus Christ our Savior (Titus 3:4-6).

Jesus Christ is the only Person who loves us regardless of how we act. His acceptance is unconditional. Therefore, regardless of what we do, His love never changes. Nothing you or I do can make Him love us any more or any less. His love is constant. This kind of love characterizes pure passion.

Look up the word *passion* in any dictionary. In addition to the phrases "strong desire" and "intense emotional excitement," you will find the phrase "the sufferings of Jesus Christ upon the cross."[1] How does Christ's crucifixion define pure passion? To answer that question, we must recognize why Jesus died for us.

> ...fixing our eyes on Jesus, the author and perfecter of faith, who for the joy set before Him endured the cross, despising the shame, and has sat down at the right hand of the throne of God (Hebrews 12:2).

This verse reveals that pure passion is composed of three elements. Let's take a moment to examine each one and understand its significance to the longing of our hearts.

Christ Initiates Love

Why did Jesus have to endure the pain and shame mentioned in Hebrews 12:2? He died on the cross because God wanted a relationship with you and me. But we couldn't reach Him. Every human is born with sin and that sin, separated us from God. Thus, if we were ever going to enjoy a meaningful relationship with God, someone besides us had to make it happen.

In love, Jesus initiated our reconciliation to God. He chose to die on the cross for us and remove our ugly sin so that our union with God could be possible. Without Christ's action, we would still be isolated from the love our hearts so desperately need.

> We love, *because He first loved us* (1 John 4:19).

> In Him we have redemption through His blood, the forgiveness of our trespasses, according to the riches of His grace (Ephesians 1:7).

Christ's initiative is an important aspect of pure passion because it signifies that He takes the lead to love us. We don't have to worry about getting His attention or keeping His approval. Neither do we have to beg, indulge, or petition Jesus. In

THE POWER OF PURE PASSION

this very moment, He is extending His love to you and me. This is a significant distinction when you consider how hard most people work to win the favor of a man or woman.

I remember in high school the frustration of trying to attract someone's interest. As a sophomore, I had a serious crush on a girl named Amy. She was tall, beautiful, and one of the smartest students in my grade. I used to sit behind her in biology class and daydream about being her boyfriend. However, I had one problem—I couldn't get her to pay attention to me. I flirted, offered to carry her books, and asked her to be my study partner. For three years I tried to earn her favor in any way possible, but all I received was an occasional hello.

In contrast, you do not have to work to gain the attention of Jesus Christ. He doesn't wait for you to grovel, plead, or show off before you can secure His interest. Instead, He makes the move to love you first. In pure passion, He died on the cross to love you, and He continues loving you for the rest of your life.

The Joy of Specific Love

Hebrews 12:2 states that joy was set before Jesus even as He endured His crucifixion. The Greek word for "joy" is *chara*, which means the "joy received from you" or "persons who are the cause of joy."[2] Applied to this verse, this definition reveals that people—including you and me—gave Jesus an underlying sense of joy during His awful torture. He was so passionate about a relationship with us that He considered His sacrifice worth the pain.

Some singles, though, doubt their worth to Jesus. As they walk in and out of church by themselves, they question whether anyone cares about them. Some churches further alienate singles by making married adults and families a priority. Many times, singles are segregated from the rest of the congregation or ignored altogether.

I experienced these feelings of loneliness and insecurity while living as a single in Atlanta, Georgia—home to several megachurches. Alone, I'd enter a sanctuary crammed with more than

2000 people and wonder whether I was just another number in God's holy herd of Christian cattle. The church wasn't necessarily to blame for my isolation. But as a single adult, I easily felt lost in the crowd. Therefore, this second aspect of Christ's passion became very important to me.

Jesus never regards you as just another face or number. He is *specifically attracted* to you and loves you as a unique person. He stated this fact when speaking to the disciples:

> What is the price of five sparrows? A couple of pennies? Yet God does not forget a single one of them. And the very hairs on your head are all numbered. So don't be afraid; *you are more valuable to Him* than a whole flock of sparrows (Luke 12:6-7 NLT).

Jesus was expressing His intimate knowledge of you. He knows every detail about you—including how many hairs are on your head and even whether your hair color is natural! You are His valuable creation. Therefore, He is attracted to you as a unique and special person.

Jesus Christ, Ruler of the universe, knows and loves you as a distinct individual. You may feel lost in the crowd, but you always stand out in the eyes of Jesus. He derives *joy* from your unique personality, your interests, your strengths, and even your weaknesses. Furthermore, He doesn't demand that you imitate other Christians to secure His approval. His love is unconditional, and He wants you to be yourself. So pure passion not only involves the initiation of Christ's love but also incorporates the truth that you are a unique individual who brings Him joy. Let's explore the third element of His passion for you.

Sacrificial Love

Though Jesus is drawn to us as individuals, His specific attraction wasn't enough to establish a holy relationship. Remember that our sin separated us from God, and we were helpless to do anything about it. Hebrews 12:2 says that Jesus "endured the cross," meaning He *sacrificed* Himself for our benefit by taking the punishment for our sin.

Christ's active participation in our messy condition is the essential element of pure passion. Notice that He did not feel attracted to us, initiate His love, and then wait for us to get our act together. Instead, He laid aside the comforts of heaven and got involved with our sin—simply for our benefit and the glory of God. His loving sacrifice on the cross made our intimate relationship with Him possible. If Jesus had not been willing to give up His life on our behalf, we would still be stuck in our sin.

It is important to note that Jesus' sacrifice was not only an act of obedience to God. He did it because He loved you so much. Christ knows that you have bad habits, selfish motives, and temper tantrums. Still, He was willing to die for you.

> Now, no one is likely to die for a good person, though someone might be willing to die for a person who is especially good. But God showed his great love for us by sending Christ to die for *us while we were still sinners* (Romans 5:7-8 NLT).

Loving a person who treats you with kindness and respect is easy. But pure passion involves the sacrifice to love someone even when he or she makes mistakes or acts selfishly. As imperfect people, we desperately need this kind of sacrificial love. Let's be honest. We both know that we sometimes act like screwups, prima donnas, or jerks. Jesus understands. He doesn't condone sinful behavior, but He doesn't reject us because of our misdeeds.

I understand if you think that the unconditional love of Christ doesn't make sense in our performance-based world. I took a while to believe that a holy God could love me regardless of my sinful behavior. Only by faith did this truth become a reality. So if you are struggling with the idea, I ask you to open your mind and consider the implications of the Bible verses you read here. Don't take my word; listen to God's Word.

Our sin did not stop Jesus from pursuing us. He *initiated* His *specific* love for us by *sacrificing* Himself for our benefit. That is pure passion—a love so deep that it fulfills our hearts for eternity.

How Does Pure Passion Affect Dating?

Maybe you are thinking, *Rob, I recognize that the love of Christ is superior to human love, but isn't this a book about dating? What does all this theology have to do with my social life? How do I experience the pure passion in dating?*

Discovering that Jesus loved me unconditionally transformed my dating life. I looked back on the struggles of my Great Dating Crusade and realized that I had set myself up for disappointment. My heart desired nutritious, unconditional love, which I thought I could find in a romantic relationship, but all I ever encountered was performance-based "chocolate." I could have dated every woman in the world without experiencing pure passion.

Instead, Jesus wanted me to understand that He already offered all the love my heart needed. I had only to accept it by faith. This meant I no longer had to seek the affection of a girlfriend or a wife to feel complete. Christ wanted to satisfy my heart.

The fact that Christ desires to fulfill our hearts does not suggest that we must avoid romantic relationships. Jesus is *not* against romance. He created it, and dating relationships are a great opportunity for His love to overflow from our hearts to those around us. Ephesians 5:2 stresses this point: "Walk in love, just as Christ also loved you and gave Himself up for us."

Christ wants to ignite within you the passionate desire to share His sacrificial love with a special person. To Jesus, dating is not about finding someone to fill your hungry heart. Rather, He intends for His love to fill you and be expressed to someone else.

I am convinced that understanding the love of Jesus Christ makes all the difference in the quality of your dating life. His love removes the hurry-up mentality to date and marry. He also frees you to be yourself around other people. And He can lead you to stop exploiting other people for your personal happiness.

Passion Awaits You

This book is an invitation to stop settling for less than what your heart truly desires. A higher love waits to take you beyond the jaded, cynical disappointments that result from most dating relationships. No longer does your heart have to survive on empty romance. You were made to experience more than just manipulation, performance, or selfish indulgence. You were created by God to share in the ecstasy of real love—not only when you get to heaven but in life on earth as well.

Before you can truly love another person, however, you must first understand how much you are already loved. So open your heart and prepare for the passion that awaits you.

Personal Bible Study

This built-in Bible study and discussion guide is designed to assist both individuals and small groups to apply the truths mentioned in this book. After you read each chapter, take some time to answer the personal Bible study questions. Then, in a group, use the discussion questions on the following page to talk about key relationship issues.

1. Read 1 John 4:10. How does this verse define love? What does this verse say about God's passionate initiative toward you?

2. Reflect on Psalm 139, focusing on verses 1-5 and 17-18. What do these verses say about God's specific love for you?

3. Turn to Colossians 1:19-23. Consider the sacrificial love that Christ demonstrated toward you. What was your original condition? What is your new condition?

4. Read John 4:6-29. Notice that the woman in the story did not deny that she had endured five unsuccessful romantic relationships (verses 17-18). What did Jesus offer this woman to fulfill her heart?

5. Have you ever had a dating relationship that initially felt like a chocolate sugar high but then suddenly crashed? What did you learn through that experience?

Group Discussion Questions

1. How is passion normally defined in our society? Why is Jesus Christ the best representation of passion?

2. Discuss three ways that men and women must perform to be accepted by each other. Why does this kind of conditional love ruin relationships?

3. Discuss the reasons why romantic human affection cannot ultimately satisfy our hearts.

4. Has Christianity been relevant to your dating life thus far? How does being a Christian help or hinder your social life?

5. Think of three examples of the media's promotion of romanticized passion. What erroneous messages does the media communicate about passion?

6. In John 6:35, Jesus said, "'I am the bread of life; he who comes to Me will not hunger.'" How does this verse apply to the hunger of your heart?

2

PASSION
FROM HEAVEN

:: :: ::

Celebrating Your Spiritual Marriage

*D*early beloved, we are gathered here today to celebrate this joyous occasion. Two people have come together, signifying their desire to be formally united in marriage. Being assured that no legal, moral, or religious barrier hinders their union, they will now join hands and answer the following questions:

Do You, Jesus Christ, take the reader of this book to be your bride? Will You love, cherish, honor, and protect this reader? Do You promise, in the presence of God and these witnesses, to be faithful to the reader for all eternity?

I do.

Do you, reader, take Jesus Christ to be your Husband? Will you take Him as the sacrifice for your sin? Will you love, cherish, honor, and worship Him? Do you promise, in the presence of God and these witnesses, to forsake all others and to rest in His love throughout eternity?

I do.

By the authority vested in Me as the Minister of the gospel and the Creator of the universe, I now pronounce you Husband and wife. What I have joined together, no man can separate.

Congratulations!

Are you a Christian single who hopes to get married? I've got great news—you are already married! You are the bride of Jesus Christ. The Bible says that the moment you accepted Him as your Savior and Lord, you were united with Him in a loving, spiritual marriage.

> For *your husband is your Maker*, whose name is the LORD of hosts; and your Redeemer is the Holy One of Israel, who is called the God of all the earth (Isaiah 54:5).

> "It will come about in that day," declares the LORD, "*that you will call Me Ishi [Husband]* and will no longer call Me Baali [Master].... *I will betroth you to Me forever;* yes, I will betroth you to Me in righteousness and in justice, in lovingkindness and in compassion, and I will betroth you to Me in faithfulness. Then you will know the LORD" (Hosea 2:16,19-20).

After the empty romances of my Great Dating Crusade, I almost gave up on the idea that true love existed. Then I discovered that being a Christian means more than just attending church, praying, or singing praise songs. As a believer in Jesus Christ, I am united with Him in an intimate relationship.

Guys, I understand that it might be difficult to picture yourself as a bride, but realize that the love of Christ transcends genders. Jesus loves a man by encouraging, empowering, and celebrating him. Likewise, He provides meaningful love to a woman through cherishing, protecting, and providing for her.

Why is it important to grasp the reality of our spiritual marriage? As we saw in the previous chapter, our hearts cannot survive solely on human relationships because human love is tied to performance. We need someone who will accept us unconditionally. Therefore, *God designed our spiritual marriage to be our primary source of love.* As our Husband, Jesus agrees to meet every need of our hungry hearts.

The Purpose of Marriage

If God intends for Christ's love to fulfill our hearts, then how do dating and marriage fit into our lives? Is God against Christian singles pursuing human relationships? The apostle Paul answered these questions in his letter to the Ephesians:

> As the Scriptures say, "A man leaves his father and mother and is joined to his wife, and the two are united into one." This is a great mystery, but it is *an illustration of the way Christ and the church are one* (Ephesians 5:31-32 NLT).

These verses state that earthly marriage illustrates the spiritual marriage that occurs between Christ and the church. God knew how difficult it would be for us to fathom our marriage to a Spirit whom we cannot see, hear, or touch. Therefore, He offers earthly marriage relationships as a physical representation of our union with Jesus.

I witnessed the power of this illustration when I attended the wedding of a friend named Kevin Lawson. As the sun set on a gorgeous October evening, Kevin stood before us ready to receive his bride, Melissa. Waiting alongside Kevin was his father, Reverend Lawson, who performed the wedding ceremony. The moment was striking because it presented a wonderful picture of the heavenly Father joining His Son, Jesus, to His bride.

As Melissa walked down the aisle in her dazzling white gown, both Kevin and his father beamed with delight. Mr. Lawson's grin was so big that he could barely contain his happiness. You could feel his excitement as he gazed upon his son and new daughter-in-law.

Kevin took Melissa's hand and lovingly recited his vows. When Kevin concluded by saying, "I do," his father joyfully blurted out, "Good!" Then, as Melissa declared her love for Kevin by stating, "I do," Mr. Lawson smiled, looked into her eyes, and said, "I am so proud of you, and I am so glad that you are a part of my family."

The happiness of Kevin's dad was undeniable. If an earthly father can feel that much excitement over his son's new bride, consider how much more delight your heavenly Father feels when you marry His Son, Jesus Christ. God is overjoyed with you as His Son's bride. Of course, Mr. Lawson knew that Melissa wasn't perfect, but he still wanted her as his daughter-in-law. In the same way, God knows that you aren't perfect, but that doesn't deter Him. He gladly welcomes you into His family.

God created earthly marriage as an illustration of our spiritual marriage to Jesus Christ. Mike Mason comments on this parallel in his book *The Mystery of Marriage:*

> To know the Lord is to be brought into a personal relationship so dramatic and overwhelming that marriage is only a pale image of it. Still, marriage is the closest analogy in earthly experience, and that is why the Bible so often uses the picture of a wedding, and of the bride and groom, to convey something of what it means for human beings to be united to God in love.[1]

When a man selects one woman to date, his pursuit mirrors the way Jesus pursues and loves you as an individual. Likewise, when a husband makes a marriage commitment to his wife, he reflects Christ's promise to never leave or forsake you (Hebrews 13:5). In addition, the intimate bliss that a husband shares with his wife portrays the delight that Christ feels toward you.

Keep in mind, however, that Jesus takes your spiritual marriage one step further by doing what no earthly spouse can—He loves you unconditionally. Men and women cannot offer each other that kind of relationship. Love between earthly spouses usually fades when difficulties arise or the happy emotions wane. In contrast, the sacrificial love of Jesus always works for your benefit—regardless of your behavior or feelings.

Your Heavenly Wedding Gifts

After Kevin and Melissa's ceremony, I spoke with Mr. Lawson and learned that in the excitement to have Melissa join his family, he arranged a special wedding present for her. The Lawson family discovered that she had been shopping for dining room chairs to use in her new home with Kevin. In a furniture store one day, Melissa noticed some elegant chairs that she thought would be perfect. But when she saw the expensive price tag, she changed her mind because she couldn't afford them. However, when the Lawsons found out, they secretly bought Melissa a set of the chairs and gave them to her as surprise wedding gifts. Melissa was completely overwhelmed by their act of love.

Did you know that when you marry Jesus, God also lavishes wedding gifts on you? In sheer joy, your heavenly Father endows you with presents to enjoy for eternity. Just as the Lawsons freely gave gifts to Melissa, God generously bestows His spiritual blessings on you. You do nothing to deserve them; you are worthy of God's gifts simply because He loves you. All He asks is that you *receive* them.

Let's discover the wedding gifts that God gives you and understand the ways they can benefit your dating life. To enhance our discussion, imagine with me that you have just recited your wedding vows with Jesus. Because you are a new member in God's family, He throws a huge wedding reception just for you. Music and joyous applause kick off the magnificent celebration. You are the center of attention as your heavenly Father cheerfully announces that He has some special gifts for you.

Wedding Gift #1: Forgiveness

God smiles as He hands you His first gift, labeled *Forgiveness*. You accept it in amazement, wondering why He would grant you such a marvelous gift. Warmly, He says, "You have no reason to ever fear Me. The punishment that your sin deserved was taken away by your Husband, Jesus."

> For Christ also died for sins once for all, the just for the unjust, so that He might bring us to God (1 Peter 3:18).

> By this will we have been sanctified through the offering of the body of Jesus Christ once for all.... "And their sins and their lawless deeds I will remember no more." Now where there is forgiveness of these things, there is no longer any offering for sin (Hebrews 10:10,17-18).

First Peter 3:18 says that Christ died once for all of your sins. So when you sin in the future, you will not need to beg God for more forgiveness.

I remember the relief I felt when God's grace became a reality to me. One day, I had repeatedly fallen into the temptation of lustful thoughts and wondered how God could continue forgiving me. Didn't His tolerance have a limit? Then, as I read the verses in Hebrews, I discovered that Christ's death on the cross satisfied the punishment for all of my sins. Regardless of the mistakes I made in life, I was forgiven. This truth did not make my lustful thoughts automatically disappear. But a transformation resulted so that I spent less time wallowing in guilt and more time responding to His love.

God forgave you once, and His forgiveness applies to your entire life—past, present, and future. He can pardon all of your sins because He is not bound by time. He already knows every future mistake that you will make. Therefore, when Jesus died for you, He paid for your future sins as well as your past ones.

How can this wonderful gift enhance your dating life? Consider that every relationship encounters conflict and disappointment. Therefore, if a couple is to maintain intimacy, their ability to forgive each other will be vital.

Hebrews 10:17 says that God will remember your sins no more. This means that He knows about your sins, but He won't dwell upon them or bring them up in the future to embarrass you. Since God gave you His forgiveness, you can extend forgiveness to the person you date when he or she offends you. You cannot love someone if you dwell upon his or her mistakes or offenses. Therefore, you have no reason to badger another person about his or her past mistakes. God forgave you and asks you to do the same with those you date. The benefit is that when people know you won't focus on their faults, they will feel safer to open up and build a deeper relationship with you.

Wedding Gift #2: Adoption into God's family

You are still in awe of God's gift of forgiveness when He quickly passes you another wedding present. It is a shiny, white certificate with your name written on it. God explains, "Since you are My Son's bride, your name is no longer Sinner. Your new name is My Beloved, Holy Child. I am so proud to adopt you into My family!" Everyone in heaven cheers and welcomes you into the family of God.

> Rejoice that your names are recorded in heaven (Luke 10:20).

> The Spirit Himself testifies with our spirit that we are *children of God*, and if children, heirs also, *heirs of God and fellow heirs with Christ*, if indeed we suffer with Him that we might be glorified with Him (Romans 8:16-17).

> So then you are no longer strangers and aliens, but you are fellow citizens with the saints, and are of God's household (Ephesians 2:19).

The significance of God adopting you into His family is that He changes your identity. Previously, you were primarily identified by your actions or occupation. For example, you might have been known as a nurse, an athlete, a lawyer, or a student. Unfortunately, you were also a sinner. Now that you are in the family of God, those occupational names are secondary, and the name "sinner" is erased. Your new identity distinguishes you as a child of God, the bride of Christ, an heir, a citizen of heaven, and a saint.

Your position in God's family enhances your dating life because it confirms that you are a lovable person. You are His holy, beloved child, so your worth no longer depends on whether you have a date on Saturday night.

This truth freed me from my self-condemnation when I couldn't get a date or when my girlfriend started to lose interest. I formerly based my worth on a woman's opinion of me. However, as I learned that God considered me a marvelous part of His family, the pressure to gain another person's approval began to dwindle.

In God's eyes, you never have a reason to consider yourself an ugly duckling. He is always proud to have you as His child. Therefore, regardless of how others treat you, you can walk with confidence that God considers you lovable and special.

Wedding Gift #3: Unconditional Acceptance

Your wedding gifts keep coming as God excitedly gives you another present marked *Unconditional Acceptance.*

> Therefore, accept one another, just as Christ also accepted us to the glory of God (Romans 15:7).

Webster's New World Dictionary says that *acceptance* means "approval." In addition, *approval* means "favorable opinion."[2] Thus, *unconditional acceptance* means that God always has a favorable opinion of you. How is this true? God accepts you because of your faith in Jesus, not because of your good behavior. You would fail miserably if you had to act perfectly all the time. Instead, God still cherishes you even when you make mistakes. Furthermore, you do not shock God when you sin. He knows every move that you will make, so your choices to sin cannot remove His acceptance.

Therefore there is now no condemnation for those who are in Christ Jesus (Romans 8:1).

God was in Christ reconciling the world to Himself, *not counting their trespasses against them,* and He has committed to us the word of reconciliation (2 Corinthians 5:19).

God does not judge Christians by their behavior. Sadly, some believers worry that God will not like them if they do not read their Bibles every morning, pray every day, tithe, and work feverishly in the church. Consequently, their fears ruin their Christian life because *people cannot love someone whom they fear.* Fear destroys intimate relationships.

I used to feel afraid of God whenever I failed to read my Bible in the morning. I worried whether His anger might cause me to wreck my car that day or lose my girlfriend. I remained in that tense state until I read my Bible at least three mornings in a row. I thought that I had to earn God's favor, and this spiritual superstition controlled my life.

However, Romans 8:1 says that when you marry Jesus, there is no condemnation for you. This means that no matter how you behave, God will always love and accept you. If you choose to sin, you will experience the natural consequences. But your deeds do not change His opinion of you. *You can do nothing to make God love you any more or any less.*

When you require people to earn your acceptance, you destroy their freedom to be themselves. Yet God accepts you unconditionally. Applying His gift to your life helps you to accept people as they are rather than demand that they please you.

For example, ladies, have you ever pressured a guy to agree with your opinion, behave more spiritually, or buy you something to keep you happy? Likewise, guys, have you ever bugged a woman to dress differently or kiss you goodnight to appease you?

God's gift of acceptance can benefit your dating life by reducing your desire to manipulate other singles. As you rest in

His favor, you can appreciate the person you date rather than coerce him or her to make you happy. With this supportive attitude, you can encourage people to be themselves and foster better relationships.

Wedding Gift #4: The Life of Christ

You are still in shock over God's generosity when He hands you yet another present, this one labeled *The Life of Christ*. You stated in your wedding vows your need for Christ, so this gift allows Jesus to live directly through you.

God knows that your life is filled with circumstances and temptations that you cannot handle. Your spiritual Husband, however, walked the earth for 33 years. During that time, He depended upon God completely, loved everyone He met, and never sinned. Through your union with Christ, Jesus wants to live His love and wisdom through your heart and mind.

> Jesus answered and said to them, "If anyone loves Me, he will keep My word; and My Father will love him, and *We will come to him and make Our abode with him*" (John 14:23).

> *For the love of Christ controls us,* having concluded this, that one died for all, therefore all died; and He died for all, so that *they who live might no longer live for themselves, but for Him who died and rose again on their behalf* (2 Corinthians 5:14-15).

> I have been crucified with Christ; and it is no longer I who live, but Christ lives in me; and the life which I now live in the flesh I live by faith in the Son of God, who loved me and gave Himself up for me (Galatians 2:20).

If you wondered how you would control your behavior as the bride of Christ, here is your answer—you can't. Your human willpower is tainted by sin. (True, some people have more self-discipline than others, but everyone eventually burns out.) You can rededicate yourself over and over, but your weak self-control will never make you a better person. To fix the problem, God allows you to exchange your inadequate willpower for the perfect life of His Son. Jesus referred to this when He said, "Take My yoke upon you and learn from Me, for I am gentle and humble in heart, and you will find *rest* for your souls" (Matthew 11:29). Yet the rest He promises occurs only when we give up. We can prevent Jesus from living through us if we choose to depend upon our own strength. Steve McVey elaborates on this point in his book *Grace Walk:*

> A real barrier preventing Christians from enjoying the rest that Jesus promised is self-effort. Many have been so conditioned to believe that they must "do something for God" that they are constantly struggling to do more and more. Many have rededicated self to God again and again. Yet self is what stands in the way of victorious Christian living. As long as we struggle to live the Christian life, Christ is hindered from living it through us.[3]

Like me, do you sometimes struggle to demonstrate mature behavior in your relationships? If so, your heavenly Father invites you to relax and let the love of Christ control you (2 Corinthians 5:14). Jesus does *not* want to help you be patient, kind, or forgiving. *Jesus wants to live His patience, kindness, and forgiveness through you.* There is a major difference between these.

It's not your job to muster up sacrificial love for someone. Jesus wants to give you His desires to love, accept, and respect another person. The question is, will you let Him?

Jesus asks you to relinquish your agenda and embrace the loving plans He has for your life. This might mean postponing your dating activity until the right time or letting go of the dream to marry a millionaire or a supermodel. Don't worry. Christ always leads you to what is best for you (Romans 8:28). As we will discuss later in this book, your Husband wants to assume responsibility for your life. So why struggle when you can rest?

Wedding Gift #5: Freedom from Sin

Your wedding celebration rolls on as God passes you another present, this one labeled *Freedom from Sin*. This gift deals with the sinful nature you possessed before you became a Christian. When you were born, you inherited the sin that Adam and Eve passed to every generation (Romans 5:12). When you marry Jesus, however, God removes your old nature and replaces it with Christ's holy nature. Therefore, the authority that sin previously had over you is now dead.

> Our old sinful selves were crucified with Christ so that sin might lose its power in our lives. We are no longer slaves to sin. *For when we died with Christ we were set free from the power of sin.* And since we died with Christ, we know we will also share his new life.... So you should consider yourselves dead to sin and able to live for the glory of God through Christ Jesus (Romans 6:6-8,11 NLT).

> He personally carried away our sins in his own body on the cross so we can be dead to sin and live for what is right. You have been healed by his wounds! (1 Peter 2:24 NLT).

Before you married Jesus, sin had control over your destiny and your behavior. As Christ's bride, however, you are dead to sin's power over you. No longer do you have to give in to evil temptations. Sure, sin will still try to lure you with unholy thoughts and selfish impulses, but now you have a choice: You can yield to temptation as before, or you can ask Jesus to live His self-control through you. Jesus was tempted but never sinned, so He can give you the wisdom and restraint to stand firm against temptation. He reminds you that the pleasure of sin is temporal and harmful to your heart, but the pleasure of your spiritual marriage fulfills you forever.

Consider the impact that freedom from sin has on your dating relationships. Whenever you feel tempted to quarrel, go overboard sexually, or cheat on someone, you have a defense against those desires. You have a source of self-control available through Jesus simply by believing in faith that it is yours. He can overcome sin's influence by motivating you to act in love, peace, and patience. We will examine further the application of this truth in chapters 6 and 8. For now, rejoice in the freedom from sin that your heavenly Husband has made possible.

Wedding Gift #6: Completeness

Staring in disbelief at your wedding gifts, you wonder if the joy will truly last. Your heavenly Father reads your thoughts, puts His arm around you, and whispers, "I know you may feel uncertain about the future of your marriage to My Son. Do not be afraid. To ease your mind, I have one more wedding gift for you. It is called *Completeness*, which is My guarantee that Jesus will eternally satisfy your heart. You will always be loved, forgiven, accepted, and considered special."

> And *in Him [Jesus] you have been made complete*, and He is head over all rule and authority (Colossians 2:10).

> Now may the God of peace Himself sanctify you entirely; and may your spirit and soul and body be preserved *complete*, without blame at the coming of our Lord Jesus Christ (1 Thessalonians 5:23).

Completeness means that you do not need to attain anything else to mature as a Christian. As Christ's bride, you will mature as you learn to apply by faith the wedding gifts that God has already given you. For instance, being a Christian for 20 years doesn't increase the likelihood that you will act patiently toward your date. Consistent patience will occur as you trust Jesus to live His patience through you.

In addition, completeness signifies that you already have everything you need through the love of Christ. No longer do you need to try to find happiness in a romantic relationship, a spouse, a child, or a new house. Those earthly things come with frustrations, and their satisfaction is short-lived. On the other hand, Jesus freely provides you with everything that you need to enjoy life, endure difficulties, and love other people (2 Peter 1:3-9).

Our society idolizes romance, companionship, and sex. Thus, we might tend to overlook the superior love that Christ offers. God is pleased when two people unite as husband and wife, but He never intended for earthly marriage to fulfill us. Instead, the marriage of a man and woman illustrates the spiritual passion we experience only with our true Husband, Jesus Christ.

Enjoy Your Wedding Gifts

Why is grasping the tangible benefits of your spiritual wedding gifts so important? Author Bob George suggests the answer in his book *Growing in Grace.*

> Our relationship to God carries over directly into our human relationships. We will ultimately treat others in exactly the same way we think God treats us.[4]

This statement had a profound impact on my life. I realized that accepting others is difficult when you believe that God is displeased with you. For instance, when I mistakenly believed that God judged me by my behavior, I usually pressured my girlfriend to please me. However, when I discovered that God unconditionally accepted me, I became less judgmental toward the women I dated. My demands diminished for a woman to constantly look her best or stay in a playful mood. I learned to let people be themselves, and I stopped fixating on my happiness.

This is just one example of how your spiritual wedding presents can have a tangible impact on your dating life. Yet you cannot benefit from your gifts until you receive them and use them by faith. If you leave them wrapped in their boxes, they won't do you any good.

Furthermore, God does not want you to hoard your wedding gifts. He intends for His generous blessings to overflow into your dating relationships. But loving another person in a godly manner cannot occur until God's love is real to you. Thus, as you begin to bask in the joy of your spiritual marriage, you can positively face the next chapter's question: Will I ever find marriage on earth?

Personal Bible Study

1. Read Isaiah 54:5-10. Who is your true Husband? What do His promises of compassion, lovingkindness, and peace indicate about your relationship with Him?

2. Turn to Hebrews 8:10-12. God says that He will write His laws on your heart and remember your sins no more. How do these two statements influence the way you treat someone on a date?

3. Read 2 Peter 1:3-9. In verse 9, Peter states that those who lack the character qualities listed have forgotten about God's forgiveness of their sin. Why is God's forgiveness a crucial element to godly dating behavior?

4. Reflect on Romans 8:14-17. Write down what it means to you to be considered a precious child in God's family.

5. Read Revelation 19:7-9 and meditate on the reality of your spiritual marriage to Jesus Christ.

6. Read 1 Corinthians 13:4-8. Then rewrite these verses, substituting the word *love* with the word *God*. Since God is love (1 John 4:8), the rewritten verses describe how God acts toward you.

Group Discussion Questions

1. Let each person in your group share which of God's wedding gifts impacts his or her life the most and why.

2. Discuss what it means to be married to Jesus Christ and the different ways His love affects you as a man or a woman.

3. How does our society devalue earthly marriage? How does marriage illustrate Christ's union with the church?

4. The Bible says God has forgiven all of your sins (past, present, and future). How does this truth influence your dating life?

5. Discuss the relational benefits of Christ living His life through you (God's Wedding Gift #4).

6. What are the differences between an earthly husband and Christ, your spiritual Husband?

3

WHERE'S THE PASSION?

:: :: ::

Dealing with the Pressure to Get Married

*A*s a single, have you often been asked, "When are you ever going to get married?" Most of us endure this frustrating inquisition from friends and relatives. They insist that "a nice person like you should settle down and start a family." Their remarks can make you feel uncomfortable about not being married.

I had a friend in his mid-thirties whose family constantly badgered him about his stagnant dating life. To stop their persecution, he had someone take pictures of him standing next to smiling women. Then he would show the photos to relatives and explain that his social life was just fine.

My buddy's situation reflects the myth that if you are not married, something is wrong with you. Besides making annoying comments, family members, the media, and many churches put pressure on singles to hurry up and become a party of two. Combine these demoralizing statements with periods of boredom or loneliness, and living single can be downright depressing. Therefore, it is not surprising that many individuals become obsessed with getting married.

In the previous chapter, we discovered the good news that we are already married to Jesus Christ. His passion is meant to be our primary source of love. But as you live out that truth, what do you do with your desires to find an earthly mate? How do you handle watching other couples enjoy romance? Do you wonder when your turn will come? Are you supposed to wait patiently for God to bring a mate to your doorstep? We will discuss questions like these in this chapter.

What Causes Our Social Suffering?

Throughout my early twenties I frequently prayed for a wife because I assumed that God's sovereignty determined the fate of my love life. But as my bachelor days turned into years, I wondered if God had forgotten about me or had denied my request because of my sin. My discontent only increased as most of my friends got married. I felt that life was passing me by.

I contended that God was unfair until He revealed the error in my thinking. One day, while reading *No Longer a Victim* by Malcolm Smith, I recognized that God's sovereignty was not the reason for my dating problems.

> Why does God allow the tragedies of life? There is no answer to that question—because it is the wrong question. Man is responsible for all wickedness, not God.... We must come to terms with the reality that life in a sinful world is not fair. The hurt that comes into your life is, at best, the fallout of a bent society disobeying God; at worst, it is evil men, out of the evil of their hearts, deliberately doing things to hurt you.
>
> God made mankind in His image and likeness, and the awesome reality of our free will is at the heart of what that means.... To take away our free will would be the end of the human race. We would then be robots—God's puppets. What we [wrongly] want is for God to take away other people's free wills—and we can be sure there are people who are praying that God will take away ours.[1]

I had mistakenly blamed God for my relational misfortune, but it wasn't His fault. My social suffering was the result of sin—mine and everyone else's. God had not unfairly assigned me to the single life. The loneliness, rejection, and heartbreak I had experienced were the results of living in a sinful world.

I realized that painful circumstances come from Satan and human sin. These calamities can strike people regardless of whether they cause it. For example, tragedies such as diseases, terrorist attacks, or natural disasters sometimes strike innocent people (Job 1:12-19; 2:7). In contrast, tribulations such as divorce, heartache, or abuse occur when people choose to hurt someone. Yet no matter how suffering happens, it always traces back to the original sin of Adam and Eve. Their mistake and its repercussions affect every generation (1 Corinthians 15:21-22).

When I was unaware of this truth, I wanted God to use His sovereignty to shield me from relational pain and bring me a perfect mate. This was an unrealistic expectation. *Though God is in control of everything, He does not divinely intervene just to make our lives easy.* He had no intention of making a beautiful woman magically appear and fall in love with me. Instead, God wanted to use His power to mature me into the kind of man that a woman would desire to marry. To achieve this goal, God had to teach me to initiate His sacrificial love toward other people. There is no doubt that God governs the universe. Psalm 37:23 says, "The steps of a man are established by the LORD." Yet He is so powerful that though He allows you to choose, He still works the outcome for His glory.

Our capacity to choose is known as *free will,* and we need this freedom to experience true love. Love exists only when a choice exists; if we are forced to love someone, then we are under manipulation. Therefore, free will is significant. *True love cannot occur unless two people freely choose to love each other.* If one person feels coerced by the other, neither of them will enjoy being together.

God wanted a relationship with you based on true love. For that reason, He gave you the freedom to decide to love Him. If you couldn't decide for yourself, you would be merely a robot, programmed as a servant or a slave. Yet God wouldn't feel any pleasure if the only love He received came from lifeless robots. Therefore, He gives you and me a free will and delights when we sincerely choose to love Him.

I recognized the importance of this truth when I couldn't get a date for my junior high school prom. I had asked several girls, but they all turned me down. Four days before the big dance, a friend told me about a girl named Tiffany who needed a date. Frankly, I wasn't attracted to her, but I asked her anyway because she was my only option. During the prom, Tiffany and I attempted to be cordial, but it was obvious that neither of us had any interest in each other. We didn't dance, and I had to fake a smile when we had our pictures taken. Most of the evening, we sat in silence and stared at the students we really liked. Through that ordeal, I learned that love cannot exist unless both parties freely choose to be together.

God created our hearts with a longing for someone to desire us. That's why we hope to find a person who is overjoyed to be with us. We don't want to date someone who simply agrees to go along for the ride. We crave intimate relationships in which others feel exhilaration when they are with us. Anything less eventually feels meaningless to our hearts. We want someone to freely choose to love us, just as God desired for mankind to freely choose Him. Through God's gift of free will, we get the opportunity to experience genuine love.

However, since God lets you decide whom you will love, He also lets you decide how you will behave. If you wish, you can treat someone with respect, patience, and humility. Or you can be prideful, insensitive, or manipulative. And if you choose to behave selfishly, you might not get a date or get married. Just like you, other people do not appreciate someone trying to take advantage of them.

Consequently, the quality of your social life is a combination of the choices you make and the decisions of those around you. For example, if a guy intentionally acts rudely, he will cause women to lose interest in him. And if he is kind, he still has no guarantee that any women will choose to show an interest in him.

You cannot control how other people treat you; you can only control how you treat others. You may choose to hurt someone, or someone may harm you. Regardless of who provokes the pain, relational problems always originate from human sin, not from God. Furthermore, you cannot expect God to prevent people from using their free will to hurt you. *If God prevented people from mistreating you, then He would also have to remove your free will to prevent you from mistreating others.*

God is holy and loving; therefore, He does not instigate breakups, abuse, or divorce (Malachi 2:16). However, He does allow humans the freedom to act selfishly. Thus, loneliness, heartache, and manipulation can enter our lives. Possessing a free will is an amazing privilege because we get to experience true love. We can abuse it, however, when we choose to sin against others.

Amazingly, God does not leave us to suffer in the relational misery we cause. Instead, He becomes our Hero by involving Himself in our troubles and working them for our good. Malcolm Smith comments,

> Does God stand helpless before the evil designs of wicked men? No! The miracle is that He actively works His love agenda within the evil choices of men and, as we place our trust in Him, He achieves His end in our lives. As the God of all love, His active energy of love is limitlessly seeking to turn every free choice we make, as well as every free choice made against us, to our highest good and His glory.[2]

God loves you so much that He immerses Himself in every detail of your life. When troubles arise, He offers to comfort you and work the situation to mature your character. Even when you decide to sin, God will not reject you. He remains patient with your stubbornness and waits until you are ready to listen. Then, the moment you seek Him, He embraces you with tenderness, acceptance, and hope. He is a relentless Optimist who "causes all things to work together for good to those who love God, to those who are called according to His purpose" (Romans 8:28). This is why our heavenly Father deserves our utmost praise.

God's Involvement in Dating

If your freewill choices determine the quality of your social life, then what is God's involvement in dating? Are you on your own to find intimacy with another person? No, the Bible says that God is active in two distinct ways.

First, God uses His sovereign control to bring people across your path. This does not suggest that you can be lazy and wait for someone to seek you out. On the contrary, you must be willing to get out and interact with people. As you do, God will guide your steps to create opportunities for new relationships. This truth is confirmed in Ephesians 2:10, in which the apostle Paul says we were "created in Christ Jesus for good works, *which God prepared beforehand that we would walk in them.*" You will meet people in the future and have the choice to date them.

Second, God not only brings people across your path but also creates the desire within you to love those people. Paul wrote in Philippians 2:13, "*For it is God who is at work in you,* both to will and to work for His good pleasure." As you get to know other singles, God moves within your heart to offer respect, kindness, and sacrifice. As you act upon His desires, you express love to another person. If that individual decides to reciprocate, then a new relationship is born.

What about those times when you experience what I call a "dating famine"? You aren't meeting any new people, and you haven't had a relationship in a long time. Does this mean that God is calling you to a life of singleness or celibacy? Are you supposed to kill your heartfelt desire for an intimate relationship in order to please God? I used to agonize over these questions until I realized that I had misunderstood God's purpose for marriage.

We discussed in the previous chapter that God created earthly marriage as a physical illustration of our spiritual marriage to

Jesus. When one man pursues one woman and commits to sacrificially loving her, we see a picture of Christ sacrificing Himself for the church. Therefore, God deems earthly marriage as both good and honorable.

> ...marriage...which God has created to be gratefully shared in by those who believe and know the truth. For everything created by God is good (1 Timothy 4:3-4).
>
> Marriage is to be held in honor among all (Hebrews 13:4).

Many singles, however, worry over their desire for marriage when they hear Bible verses that say "it is better not to marry" (Matthew 19:10-12; see 1 Corinthians 7:8,25-40). Some think that God considers singleness a holier way of life. That is not true. In every case, the scriptural suggestion to remain single refers to people in periods of distress, eunuchs, or those who choose not to marry. In these instances, the desire to remain single is a special gift from God (1 Corinthians 7:7).

Sometimes God calls someone to pursue a special ministry, unencumbered by a relationship. To assist that person, He places an unmistakable urge within him or her to stay single. This desire may be temporary or last forever. In either case, this gift frees an individual from distraction and allows that person to maximize his or her effectiveness in a particular ministry. A modern example might be a missionary who wants to serve in a remote region where taking a spouse and children would be unmanageable. In that situation, God gives a person a special contentment to decline marriage. Other examples include monks, nuns, priests, or anyone who prefers to serve the Lord without a relationship distracting them.

If you do not want to stay single, you do not dishonor God. Instead, He gifted you with the passion to share His love with someone else. To assist you, God will bring people across your path, and He will work within you to love someone. If it leads to marriage, that's fine. If it doesn't, that's okay as well. Remember that you are already complete in your marriage to Christ.

Your Involvement in Dating

God works on your behalf to help you meet and love other people. However, you determine whom you accept and whom you reject. As you interact with another single adult, you have the freedom to decide which direction your relationship will take. You can choose to become romantic with someone, be friends only, or end your time together. In addition, the other person also has a say in the matter, which means he or she gets to influence the outcome as well. Consequently, a relationship will not exist unless both of you decide to love each other. If you or the other person make sinful decisions, your social life can be impaired.

You may deeply desire marriage, but the consequences of living in a fallen world can prevent you from reaching that goal. For instance, the person you want to date may ignore you, an illness may hinder you, or, as in my case, someone you love may decide to desert you. The sins of humanity create numerous barriers to good relationships.

God constantly encourages Christian singles to love each other, but He also allows their selfish actions to tear each other apart. He permits this tribulation so that everyone can keep his or her free will. Without it, none of us would ever experience true love. Therefore, our involvement in dating revolves around deliberately deciding to love another person. We can improve our dating opportunities by choosing to sacrificially love people. Or we can opt for selfish behavior and destroy our relationships.

Your future is in God's hands, but He does not promise you marriage. Finding a spouse is a free-will process in which two people decide to sacrifice themselves for each other's benefit. Marriage is not some predetermined process that happens mysteriously. You will become very frustrated if you think that God mystically pairs people up. He does not unite people by overriding their minds and wills. God brings people together and encourages them to love one another but lets them decide their relational future.

Drop the Demand

Jennifer was a disgruntled single woman at my church. She was 36 years old and complained that her life was slipping away. Six years had passed since her last boyfriend, and her dating life remained in limbo. Jennifer wondered whether her heart still had the capacity to love. Beneath her jaded disposition festered an undercurrent of resentment toward God.

After attending church regularly for more than two years, she suddenly disappeared. Three months later, I bumped into her at a restaurant and asked her whether she had moved to another church. She replied, "No, I've quit church altogether. I just can't bring myself to worship a God who would leave me in such loneliness." Jennifer concluded that if she was ever going to serve the Lord again, He'd better bring her a husband—and fast.

Have you ever felt as Jennifer did? Do you get mad at God because you are single? Have you placed a secret demand on Him to bring you a spouse? If so, I know how you feel. Suffering the loss of one marriage, and after repeated attempts at dating, I was very discontent by the age of 30. I longed for marriage but couldn't seem to grab it.

Whenever I felt particularly upset about being single, I sat in my den recliner and griped to God about the injustice of my social life. He expressed His mercy by allowing me to continue living despite some of the things I yelled at Him. I knew that my freewill decisions influenced my relationships. But the process of dating was so frustrating that I wanted God to make marriage happen. I knew He had the power, so expecting a wife from Him seemed logical.

When I demanded that God rush me a spouse, He usually replied with a question: "*Rob, is the love of Jesus Christ enough for you? Have you allowed His complete forgiveness and unconditional acceptance to satisfy your heart?*

In tears of resignation, I would admit, "No, Lord, I want marriage more than I want You." I still believed that to feel complete, my heart needed the affection of a woman.

One day, God gently reasoned with me. *Rob, you've had more than 20 dead-end dating relationships and a wife who deserted you. Can't you see that human love is conditional? My love for you is the only thing that you can count on.*

Suddenly, something within my mind clicked. I responded, "Lord, You are right. Why am I chasing marriage when it can't give the perfect love that my heart craves? Only You offer everything I need." So on April 20, 1998, sitting in my recliner, I relinquished to God my demand to get married. I still wanted to find a wife someday, but I no longer considered marriage necessary to complete my life. If I remained single until I died, that was okay—God promised to fulfill my heart.

When we demand that God bring us a mate, we block His love from enhancing our social life. The anger that we harbor builds a wall between Him and us. If we are honest with ourselves, we realize that our demand for marriage is a refusal of God's love because we want our selfish desires met. God will never stop loving us, but we ignore Him when we desperately seek a human being to make us happy. Furthermore, whatever we depend upon for our happiness winds up controlling us. If we believe that we need a boyfriend or girlfriend to be satisfied, then people, rather than God, will control our lives.

Use the following questions to consider whether you might want marriage more than you want God:

- Am I dating to find someone who can make me feel better about myself?
- Can I feel content and thankful to God in my singleness?
- Am I cynical about relationships with the opposite sex?
- Am I afraid of the possibility of never getting married?

Friend, do not let the goal of marriage manipulate you. You will become miserable because you cannot completely control the outcome. (Remember that marriage also requires another person to choose you.) More importantly, marriage cannot fulfill you. God's purpose for your life is not that you find a mate. Rather, His objective is to lead you to share His sacrificial love with other people (Romans 12:1; Hebrews 13:16). However, His love cannot benefit your relationships until you surrender your right to get married. I'm not saying you must sign up to become a monk or a nun. Instead, when you surrender your rights, you allow your loving, spiritual Husband to guide your life. He wants to satisfy your heart with His love and let it overflow into your relationships.

Giving Jesus Christ supervision of your life is sometimes called *brokenness*, which means coming to the end of yourself. Brokenness occurs when you give up trying to make life work in your own strength. With an attitude of humility, you relinquish your rights and selfish demands to Christ (Luke 9:23-24).[3] In other words, Jesus breaks off the bad stuff. When you are broken, you cease struggling to get what you want. You become open to Christ's purposes and allow Him to live His passionate life through you. In that regard, yielding your rights to Him is the best decision that you could ever make.

Once you surrender your demand for marriage, Christ can motivate you to date for the right reasons. But don't expect your love life to automatically blossom. Jesus may urge you to postpone dating if the time is not right or if you are still focused on yourself. Don't dismay, though; taking a break doesn't necessarily mean that you will remain by yourself forever. The pause is for your good. Wait on Him, and at the proper time He will encourage you to renew romance—when it is most beneficial for you.

A New Cycle of Relationships

If you crave marriage above everything else, then acceptance by the opposite sex will control your self-esteem. Your vulnerable heart will remain unhealthy because you cannot control whether other people accept you. No matter how hard you work to keep someone happy, sinful imperfections will always complicate your relationship. Thus, as long as you expect dating to fulfill your heart, you will stay in this vicious circle:

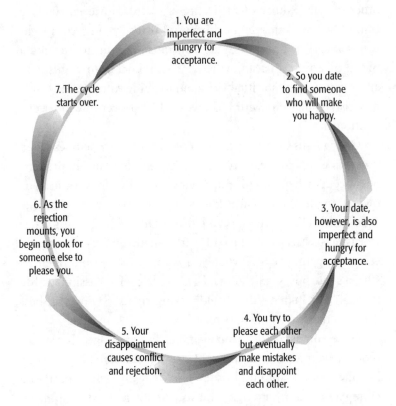

1. You are imperfect and hungry for acceptance.

2. So you date to find someone who will make you happy.

3. Your date, however, is also imperfect and hungry for acceptance.

4. You try to please each other but eventually make mistakes and disappoint each other.

5. Your disappointment causes conflict and rejection.

6. As the rejection mounts, you begin to look for someone else to please you.

7. The cycle starts over.

This simple diagram depicts why many dating singles jump from one relationship to another. They require more happiness or fulfillment than their dates can give. Initially, they enjoy being with someone new, but mistakes and imperfections inevitably cause disappointment. As their contentment wanes, they end the relationship and look for someone else to make them happy. Sadly, they will search forever because God never created dating or marriage to satisfy their hearts.

Let me emphasize that God does not deny our need for loving, human relationships. We were not designed to live as hermits or loners. We were born with a need to connect intimately with other people. Nevertheless, God does not want us to shortchange our hearts by making imperfect human relationships our primary source of acceptance, purpose, or significance. As we saw in chapter 1, God wants romance to serve as the chocolate dessert after we nourish our hearts on a steady diet of Christ's passionate love. In other words, *dating is a means to express the love that Christ has already given us.* This is what the Lord implied when He said, "From his innermost being shall flow rivers of living water" (John 7:38). We receive from Christ the love we need; then we give that love to someone else in dating.

Please do not misunderstand me. God established romance as a wonderful blessing. But we jeopardize the welfare of our hearts when we consider human affection mandatory for our self-worth. Only Christ's unconditional acceptance can complete us. When you receive the love of Christ and let it overflow into a romantic relationship, a new cycle of dating can occur:

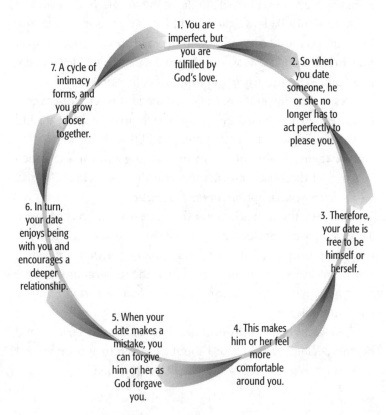

1. You are imperfect, but you are fulfilled by God's love.

2. So when you date someone, he or she no longer has to act perfectly to please you.

3. Therefore, your date is free to be himself or herself.

4. This makes him or her feel more comfortable around you.

5. When your date makes a mistake, you can forgive him or her as God forgave you.

6. In turn, your date enjoys being with you and encourages a deeper relationship.

7. A cycle of intimacy forms, and you grow closer together.

God Initiates—We Respond

Earlier in the chapter, we mentioned two ways that God gets involved with dating. First, He works to bring people across your path. Second, He initiates the desire within you to love people. He puts His desires within you—He makes them a part of you.

Hebrews 13:21 says God will "equip you in every good thing to do His will, *working in us* that which is pleasing in His sight, through Jesus Christ." Notice that God works to provide you with the motivation to do His will. Since your spiritual marriage unites you with Christ, God can shape the desires within your mind and heart (1 John 4:15-16). Let me illustrate the process of Jesus working within us to initiate a new dating relationship.

Three months after I surrendered my right to marriage, I felt restless and wanted to meet some new singles. *(This was Christ initiating the process.)* I wasn't in the mood to date, but my current circle of friends had dwindled, and I felt as if I was in a social rut. One day, I received information in the mail about a beach retreat for Christian singles. As soon as I read the pamphlet, I felt a desire to attend. *(This was Christ planting His desires in me.)*

Despite the inspiration, I rejected the idea when I discovered that over 600 people had signed up. The thought of being around that many singles intimidated me. In addition, I did not wish to endure their scrutiny of me in my bathing suit on a crowded beach. So I threw the information into the trash can. *(This was Christ letting me choose out of my free will.)*

However, the urge to attend this retreat would not go away. Though I tried, I couldn't deny that it was a great opportunity to meet new people. *(This was Jesus reasoning within my heart.)* For 12 weeks I wavered on going, but as the registration deadline grew near, my interest began to peak. *(Jesus was continuing to encourage me.)*

Two weeks before the deadline, I had lunch with a friend, and he unexpectedly said, "I heard about a beach retreat coming up. I don't want to go alone. Would you like to join me?"

Knowing that my buddy wanted to go suddenly removed my reluctance. I immediately responded, "Sure, that sounds great." *(This was Jesus using His power to bring someone across my path, prompting me to make a decision!)*

Needless to say, Christ's urgings were for my benefit. The retreat turned out to be a lot of fun. Throughout the weekend, I met many new people and started some new friendships, particularly with a beautiful girl named Ashley. Because of Christ working within me, I returned home with a reinvigorated social life.

Jesus wants you to enjoy love with other people. He is wiser than you are, however, so He wants to oversee your dating life and direct you into beneficial relationships. He cannot do that until you surrender your relational rights and follow the desires He puts within your heart. I encourage you to take that step today.

No Formula for Marriage

Two fallacies keep many singles from experiencing a passionate dating relationship. The first fallacy assumes that God has one special person waiting for you. All you need is faith, and God will do the rest. This notion always leads to pressure and frustration.

For example, if you think God has someone hidden somewhere in the world for you to find, then you may wonder, *Where is this person, and why hasn't God brought him or her to me yet?* You might even speculate, *Is God mad at me? Did I miss this individual earlier in life and lose my chance at true love?* Thoughts like these cause feelings of fear, anxiety, and even anger toward God rather than peace and contentment.

On the other hand, some singles believe that the secret to getting married is to deny your desire for it altogether. I've heard this misconception promoted by married people who claim they met their spouses soon after they stopped looking for one. This implies that God will bring you a mate as soon as you stop desiring marriage. That theory is ridiculous. God does not play cat-and-mouse games with you or make you jump through hoops to appease Him. Neither is He a heavenly vending machine that you must pay to receive a blessing. God blesses you without reserve (Ephesians 2:8-9).

Some people find spouses when they aren't looking because *they appear more attractive when they are relaxed and unselfish.* Their composed demeanor reflects maturity and the ability to love others. No one wants to date someone who is anxious or self-focused. People can sense when someone is desperate. Smart singles keep their eyes open for those who seem to be content with where God has them. That way, they lessen the risk of dating someone who will try to manipulate them.

No formula exists for finding a mate. As we have discussed, marriage occurs when two people meet and both choose in their free will to love each other sacrificially.

Let Jesus Improve Your Love Life

If you are single, please do not believe the worldly lie that something is wrong with you. In the eyes of Christ, you are not a social outcast. Jesus considers you lovable, interesting, victorious, and holy—and His opinion is the only one that matters. However, keep in mind that fascinating things can happen when the love of Christ becomes the core of your self-esteem. Many times, you become a more attractive person to date.

Most singles prefer to date people who are content with themselves. You naturally appear more attractive when you are content in Christ. His love can work within your heart to remove the social barriers that blocked you from a passionate dating relationship. For example, resting in Christ's unconditional acceptance releases you from the pressure to perform for others. In turn, you can feel free to be yourself, which is one of the most attractive qualities you can exhibit. No one wants to date a phony. Men generally favor dating a woman who respects herself. Likewise, women usually like to date a man who feels secure. We cannot fake attitudes such as these, but we can have them when we rest in the love of Christ.

Jesus is the only Person who can fulfill your heart. As you are satisfied by your spiritual marriage to Him, you position yourself to be ready for earthly marriage. Delight in His passion, and He will lead you to love others by making His desires your desires.

Delight yourself in the LORD; and He will give you the desires of your heart (Psalm 37:4).

Personal Bible Study

1. Romans 5:12-21 says the sin of Adam was passed on to you at birth. How did Christ free you from this awful condition?

2. Read Job 1:6–2:10. Notice that God never caused any hurt to Job. Who instigated Job's tragedy? What does this mean when tribulation affects you?

3. Turn to Psalm 118:1-14 and meditate upon God's goodness toward you during a difficult circumstance.

4. Look up Proverbs 16:9 and 20:24. Consider how the Lord directs your path in life. Ask God to make you aware of opportunities that He creates for you to express love to other people.

5. In 2 Corinthians 5:14, the apostle Paul states that the love of Christ controls a Christian. Can you list two examples of how Jesus motivated you to love another person in the last week?

6. Read Luke 9:23-25 and 2 Corinthians 12:9-10. These verses describe the term "brokenness" discussed in chapter 3. Why is brokenness beneficial? Have you given up your right to marriage?

CHAPTER 3 — WHERE'S THE PASSION?

Group Discussion Questions

1. Discuss two ways that society makes singles feel inferior. How can your spiritual marriage to Christ help you disregard cultural lies?

2. Talk about how people normally react toward God when tragedy strikes or they lose a romantic relationship. Next, have someone read Romans 8:31-39 aloud. In light of these verses, how should we view God in the midst of tragedy?

3. Discuss the amazing benefits of God allowing you to have a free will. How does free will apply to your dating life?

4. Discuss why God established marriage on earth. Can you be a complete person as a single adult? Why?

5. Consider why dating relationships cannot provide you with long-term happiness.

6. Discuss two ways that knowledge of the love of Christ can make you a more attractive person to date.

Chapter 4

Choose
Your Passion

:: :: ::

Determining the Best Person to Date

*Y*ou may be familiar with an educational establishment known
as the School of Hard Knocks. As a single adult, I attended this
esteemed institution and received my doctorate in dating. It took
a lot to earn my degree, including breakups, rejections, and
broken hearts. And then I had to retake all of my classes after my
wife left me. Thankfully, God used my painful relationships to
develop my maturity. One of His best lessons was teaching me to
make wiser choices about whom I dated.

Much of my heartache stemmed from my confusion about
what to look for in a mate. Growing up, I fell for the worldly lie
that the best women were those endowed with superficial qualities, such as beauty, charm, style, humor, or athleticism. So I
sought relationships with girls who possessed these outer attributes and gave little thought to their character, selflessness, or
maturity.

In college, I was so superficial that I even developed a silly
system to decide which women to pursue. I would select a girl in
a classroom and quickly glance at her. If the glimpse of her face

electrified me three times in a row, then she became my prime dating target. However, if looking at her failed to give me a tingling sensation, I lost interest. My method may sound crude, but I assure you it was no different from what most of my friends did. Whenever we wondered whom to ask out, our final decision usually rested upon the "cuteness" factor.

Why Relationships Fall Apart

It took me 13 years of dating to finally recognize my shallow view of women. Through an epiphany, God revealed that my relationships usually started off hot but always fizzled out. He helped expose my problem through the book *Safe People* by Drs. Henry Cloud and John Townsend. The authors visited a Christian college and asked the students what qualities they desired in a potential mate. Most students wanted someone "ambitious, fun, attractive, spiritual, smart, or witty."[1]

These responses troubled Cloud and Townsend because of their experience counseling unhappily married couples. From their research, they composed a list of common reasons for marital dissatisfaction between husbands and wives. When they compared their list to the students' list of mate selection qualities, they noticed a drastic difference. Unhappy spouses usually have the following complaints about their mates:

- He doesn't listen to me.
- She is so perfect that she can't understand my struggles.
- He seems so distant that I feel alone.
- She always tries to control me.
- He makes promises but really doesn't follow through.
- He is condemning and judgmental.
- She is always angry at me for something I did or didn't do.
- I tend to be my worst self with her.
- I cannot trust him.[2]

These complaints resulted from Cloud and Townsend's work with hundreds of married couples on the verge of separation. Notice how the list of unhappy remarks has nothing to do with beauty, humor, intelligence, or wealth. Marriages do not fall apart because one spouse isn't funny enough. Neither do couples separate because one person is too smart. Marital difficulties result from deeper issues.

Relationships fall apart when two people refuse to love each other sacrificially. Selfish behavior destroys their union because intimacy cannot coexist with immaturity or a lack of character. Problems like these originate beneath the surface of a person. Therefore, though someone may look good, he or she may not necessarily be good for you. Cloud and Townsend conclude, "We choose people based on outward appearances...but then we experience the pain of being in a real relationship with them, and come up very empty-handed."[3]

All too often, singles choose whom they date by focusing strictly on outward characteristics. We know that guys can be notorious for judging a woman by her figure. Yet women do the same thing when they grade a man by his popularity, humor, or wealth. This does not mean that these visible attributes are unimportant. A person's beauty, money, and intelligence can certainly benefit a relationship.

The problem with exterior attributes, however, is that they do not reveal a complete picture of someone. In addition, external attractiveness does not indicate whether a person is mature enough to love unselfishly. Instead, people who rely too much upon their outer appearance commonly lack the ability to consider the needs of others. They become so self-absorbed that, to them, sacrifice means that someone else should concede to their wishes. This kind of attitude prevents pure passion.

My experience confirms that if you date solely for superficial reasons, you will end up in an unfulfilling relationship. I dated several girls who were beautiful, smart, and playful but had no desire to give. Rather, they always wanted me to concede. In other words, my world had to revolve around theirs. Initially, the romance felt so good that I didn't mind yielding to them. Over time, however, I became irritated because I felt as if I always had to give in.

I discovered that no matter how much pleasure, excitement, or affection a dating relationship offers, those things cannot satisfy the heart's desire to be genuinely loved. We yearn for a relationship in which we can feel celebrated by the other person. Dating is a nuisance when your boyfriend or girlfriend doesn't offer trust, cooperation, and acceptance.

Choosing Whom to Date

If external appearances do not guarantee good relationships, then how do you decide whom to date? Does God suggest settling for someone who is trustworthy but dull? No, God wants you to form relationships based on more than just piety. He wants you to choose whom you date for the same reasons that Christ chose to initiate a relationship with you: specific attraction and sacrificial love.

Let's quickly review why Jesus pursued you. In chapter 1, we discovered that Christ endured His crucifixion because He felt a specific joy toward you (Hebrews 12:2). As a unique individual created in the image of God, you captivated Him (Genesis 1:26). To Jesus, your special beauty fascinated His heart. His attraction, however, was not enough by itself to establish a holy relationship with you. Your sin stood between you and Him. To experience intimacy with you, Jesus had to sacrifice Himself on your behalf. In addition, you had to sacrifice your pride and accept Him as your Savior. Once these actions were complete, you were united with Christ in a glorious spiritual marriage.

Chapter 2 explained that God established dating and marriage as an earthly illustration to help you comprehend your spiritual union (Ephesians 5:32). Therefore, when you sacrificially love a person who specifically attracts your heart, you taste the passion that Christ feels about you. Let's explore the essence of specific attraction and sacrificial love.

The Heart of Attraction

I have always been attracted to tall, slender women with long, dark hair. As I stood waiting in a hotel lobby one day, my heart skipped a beat as she came into view. Of all the women I have ever seen, this one had it all. Waves of brunette curls swept over her shoulders, enhancing her svelte figure. I stared at her as if in a trance. Her legs were long and thin, and...whoops—she caught me looking. Busted, I glanced away, pretending not to notice her. Yet as she walked by, I thought, *Wow! Who is she, and how can I meet her?*

This happened during the singles beach retreat that I mentioned in chapter 3. God had urged me to attend so I could meet some new friends. Suddenly, I wanted to find a way to meet this gorgeous young woman. Amazingly, I had to wait only a few hours because a friend of mine invited me to join his group for dinner— and there she was.

At the restaurant that evening, I discovered that this beauty's name was Ashley. We talked, and I learned that we had similar upbringings, had both traveled overseas, and had accepted Christ at a young age. I was mesmerized as we chatted—did I mention her long dark hair?

Wouldn't dating be boring if beauty or charm didn't exist? Outward appearances are a blessing because they spark interest between two people. For instance, when a man meets a woman, their excitement about one another's appearance or personality stimulates a desire to know each other better. Of course, they eventually need to determine one another's integrity. It is difficult, however, to start a new relationship based solely on character. Virtue can take months to verify. Therefore, external attraction serves as the catalyst for people to establish new relationships.

Have you considered the specific qualities that attract you to the opposite sex? What kind of person does your heart dream about? What characteristics completely mesmerize you? Do you prefer a certain body type, height, or hair color? Do you prefer a distinct kind of laugh, hobby, interest, or personality? When you meet someone who possesses these attributes, you probably feel irresistibly drawn to him or her.

Interestingly enough, most of your relational preferences are built-in. Have you noticed that certain attributes about the opposite sex always enthrall you—regardless of how much you try to ignore or downplay them? For example, as I mentioned, I have a natural bent toward women with long brunette hair. I cannot explain why, but dark hair absolutely dazzles me. Blondes or redheads are also attractive, but when I walk into a crowded room, brunettes catch my eye first.

My innate preferences drew me to Ashley during the singles retreat. Her gorgeous dark hair drove me wild, as did her tall slender shape. She further enchanted my heart when I learned that she was a longtime Christian, loved to travel, and enjoyed athletics. Ashley attracted me so much that within two months, I felt compelled to ask her out. She also felt an attraction to me, and soon after, our relationship was born.

The Origin of Attraction

Consider the characteristics that fascinate you about the opposite sex. Where did that fascination originate? Did we secretly instruct ourselves as children to only date people with brunette hair or a witty personality? Did our parents or friends give us our tendencies as mandatory rules? No, I believe the desires within our hearts are gifts from God, designed to enlighten us about the specific attraction that Jesus feels for you and me. Bear in mind that if we did not have specific tastes in people, we could not comprehend the feeling of being loved as individuals.

Millions, perhaps billions of Christians compose the body of Christ. Yet in the midst of such a large family of believers, Jesus does not want you to forget that He loves you specifically. You are special to Him. To help you grasp His individual attraction to you, He gives you a unique assortment of preferences that attract you to a certain type of individual. If this weren't the case, then why would God go through all of the trouble to create every human being differently? He is not only displaying His creativity but also trying to teach us about His specific love.

We tend to forget that God is a romantic Person. We must remember that He is the Author of love, attraction, and sex, and we were made in His image. Thus, we should not downplay the traits that attract our hearts to the opposite sex. We should embrace our preferences and allow them to lead us into a loving relationship with someone. As we do, we receive a taste of God's unique enchantment with us.

Listen to Your Heart

Sadly, many singles ignore their heartfelt preferences because they grow up hearing that their heart is wicked. People who believe this idea use certain Scriptures to support their position, such as Jeremiah 17:9 or Mark 7:21. Yet, those verses refer to the old covenant, before Christ's death on the cross. After His death and resurrection, God established a new covenant, which allowed Christ to "dwell in your hearts through faith.... that you may be filled up to all the fullness of God" (Ephesians 3:17-19).

Before Christ died, everyone's hearts were wicked because God did not reside in them. After Christ's death and resurrection, however, He could, by your faith, cleanse your heart and live inside of your spirit (Ezekiel 36:25-26; 1 Corinthians 6:17; Galatians 2:20).

Now that Christ is within you, He puts desires into your heart that you can trust. This allows Him to guide you into new relationships. You still have the choice to sin, but sin no longer dwells within your heart. Christ kicked it out and made you a new creation, holy and righteous (2 Corinthians 5:17,21). Now that Christ lives within you, His desires can become your desires (Hebrews 10:16; Ephesians 2:10; 1 John 4:16-17). (If you wonder why you still sin, don't worry—we will discuss that issue in chapter 6.)

When Christ lives His life through you, He influences how you socialize with others. He places the urge within you to love someone genuinely and selflessly. In addition, He can impart the appropriate desires for romance. Therefore, listen to your heart and follow the impulses that Christ gives you. However, *do not* confuse His urges with the selfish desire to only date whoever "turns you on" sexually. You can get yourself into trouble when you concentrate on superficial appearances and disregard the importance of character.

God gave Jesus direct access to your heart so that He could guide you to balance romance and integrity. He wants you to be equally concerned about such things as a person's spiritual maturity, intelligence, family relationships, and work ethic. He cares about more than just the typical physical attractions between people. This does not imply that Christ will lead you to marry someone plain or boring. On the contrary, if you decide to marry, Jesus wants you to be thrilled about that person. He wants you to have a relationship that benefits your whole person. So do not settle for less than what your heart truly desires.

Guys, do you know what characteristics specifically attract you to the opposite sex? What type of woman does your heart dream about? Don't limit yourself to just body type or hair color. Consider the full range of exterior attributes and create a list that specifies such things as education level, involvement in the church, personality, family ties, energy level, goals, hobbies, or even the way she carries herself. Determine the qualities that inspire you to initiate a relationship with a woman. If you ignore your heart, you will likely miss an opportunity to initiate a passionate relationship.

Ladies, have you contemplated what your heart wishes for in a man? Besides a steady income and good looks, do you desire a guy who is laid back, easy to talk to, good with kids, solid in his career, or an active leader? Listen to your heart, make a list, and don't lower your standards just to get a date. If your dreamboat has not arrived, wait patiently and keep your eyes open. You hinder your chance for intimacy if you give yourself to a man who does not spark passion within you. Let me emphasize that dating with passion never involves pursuing someone bad for you. Infatuation or sexual chemistry may feel good, but if it becomes the driving force in your relationship, it can cause your demise. You need more than romantic excitement to experience pure passion. As we will discuss later in this chapter, great relationships center on consistent, sacrificial love.

More than Friends

Friendship is a vital aspect of dating because it provides the support, sympathy, and encouragement necessary for two people to grow together. If you are not close friends with your boyfriend or girlfriend, then you will have difficulty communicating about issues that matter to you. A relationship cannot flourish without an environment in which you can be yourself and openly discuss your thoughts. Also, friendship allows you to enjoy someone during the less than thrilling points in life. This is important because if you get married, you will experience some unexciting seasons.

On the other hand, a passionate dating relationship requires more than just friendship because Jesus loves you more than as a friend. In John 15:14, Jesus calls you His friend, but throughout most of Scripture He calls you His bride. Whenever the Bible refers to the bride of Christ, it inspires images of enchanting beauty and romantic attraction (Song of Solomon 4; Revelation 19:7-9). Therefore, if you want a relationship based on Christ's passion, settling for a platonic friendship will not suffice. Passionate dating includes the flame of a mutual, physical fascination.

Opposites Detract

Some suggest that people who are opposites make great marriage partners. This is erroneous thinking. Long-lasting relationships usually occur when two people share many similarities because similarities help create stability.

On the other hand, when a couple comes from dissimilar cultures, customs, or traditions, their differences require more compromise and adjustment. Numerous differences can create an incredible level of stress and require lots of negotiation.

When you share numerous similarities with someone, you improve your ability to develop a long-term connection. Furthermore, by viewing life in the same way, you reduce the potential for conflict. Which similarities are most helpful? Psychologists cite such issues as "intellect, spirituality, intimate verbal sharing, interests, and role expectations." The most destructive differences include "energy levels, personal habits, uses of money, and verbal skills."[4]

When you date someone drastically different from you, you usually attempt to change that person. The more you try to change someone's values, goals, or personality, the more stressful your relationship becomes. By contrast, if you share the same interests and beliefs, your relationship has a built-in basis for harmony.

If you feel drawn to date someone very different from you, be careful that you do not use him or her to complete you. For instance, a shy girl may be tempted to date an aggressive guy so that he will take care of things that intimidate her, such as negotiating and talking at parties. Likewise, a passive man may feel compelled to date an extravagant woman who will bring some excitement into his life.

In chapter 2 we discussed that your spiritual marriage to Jesus has already made you complete (Colossians 2:10). Therefore, dating someone opposite to you will not make you whole. Only the unconditional love of Christ can satisfy your heart. If you still feel that you need a person to make you complete, you haven't fully accepted His love yet. Open your heart to the reality that Jesus wants to fulfill you with His passion.

Sacrificial Love Sustains a Relationship

We've discussed how specific attraction works to initiate a relationship. Yet if you date based on outward attractions alone, you will set yourself up for failure and disappointment. Beauty and charisma cannot hold couples together when difficulties arise. To experience lasting passion, two people must be willing to *sacrifice* for each other.

Jesus demonstrated sacrificial love when He came to earth 2000 years ago. In humility, He left heaven to pursue His attraction to us, but our sin inhibited a relationship with Him. Thankfully, Jesus didn't look at our imperfections, lose interest, and go back to heaven. Instead, He gave up His life, sacrificed Himself on the cross, and established our spiritual bond. Christ forfeited His immediate happiness on earth so that we could thrive in eternal unity with Him.

In the same way, pure passion in dating cannot survive on mutual attraction alone. Sinful imperfections and selfish behavior constantly work to destroy a relationship. For two people to maintain intimate love, both parties must be willing to forfeit their desires for the profit of the other person.

I witnessed this kind of sacrificial love when my father sold his vacation home in the mountains. He had always dreamed of a private retreat where he could retire. But the home wound up becoming a burden to my mother because of its isolated location. She felt bored without the fellowship of their close friends and church community. It was a tough decision, but my father gave up his dream for the benefit of their marriage. Through that action, I realized how deeply he loved my mom.

Passionate dating occurs as two people jointly give up their wishes for the benefit of each other. Anything less is merely two people using each other for personal gain. Therefore, follow your heart to date someone who fascinates you, but do not give that person your heart until he or she exhibits a willingness to love you sacrificially.

Dating is preparation for marriage. *Marriage is a commitment to an imperfect person for his or her highest good.* This commitment includes a willingness to lay down your happiness, your wishes, and your dreams for the benefit of the other person. Marriage is mutual give and take, but many singles do not realize that sometimes one person may do most of the giving for a long period. For example, if a wife is stricken with cancer, her husband doesn't carry on with his routine. In love, he forfeits his desires to fish or play golf and changes his schedule to take care of his wife's needs. His primary focus is to support and encourage her. As he gives up his wishes for his wife's benefit, their relationship is strengthened.

You are not ready to date seriously if you are not prepared to love sacrificially. You may be old enough, charming enough, or sexy enough to attract people, but if your goal is to find someone who will make you happy, then you are dating for selfish reasons. The purpose of a romantic relationship should be to give, not to get, because your heart already has all the love it needs from Christ.

Conversely, sacrifice does not mean that you allow someone to take advantage of you. If your date insists that you do all of the giving, you probably should end your relationship. He or she is using you. Look for someone who is willing to lay down his or her wishes out of love.

The Character of Sacrificial Love

When I met Ashley, my attraction was initially based on her outward appearance and the interests that we shared in common. But having a past riddled with fruitless dating relationships and a wife who deserted me, I realized that my external fascination with a woman was no indication of relational success. My heart needed more than just a pretty face. I wanted to share lasting passion with someone. If I hoped to develop that kind of relationship with Ashley, sacrificial love would need to be present.

Sacrifice is the key to building any intimate relationship. We discern a person's willingness to sacrifice by determining his or her character. A person has character when he or she chooses to love even without receiving any immediate benefit. Unfortunately, people do not wear signs around their necks informing you that they possess honesty, loyalty, and compassion. Therefore, your job is to determine the virtue of the person that you date. Do not assume or take someone else's word on the matter. You must draw your own conclusions.

To consider the character of someone you date, review the following list of questions:

- Does my date allow our relationship to progress naturally rather than rush it?
- Does my date adapt to the situation when plans change instead of pouting?
- Does my date dress in a manner that doesn't tempt the opposite sex to lust?
- Has my date ended relationships with those who are harmful?
- Does my date forgive people when they run late or act rudely?
- Does my date make the effort to be on time?
- Does my date accept others or try to change people?
- Can my date say no to sex when other people encourage the issue?
- Does my date exhibit generosity with time and money to those in need?
- Does my date care for someone even when the person is sick or depressed?

This list of questions shows that character centers on seeking the overall benefit of another person. Sometimes that includes telling someone no, such as when you are tempted to go too far sexually, waste money, or spend all of your time together. A person's integrity is determined by whether he or she can ignore his or her pride, delay immediate gratification, and consider what is best for someone else.

Discovering Ashley's character was my primary focus when we began dating. Jesus urged me to look past her outer qualities and determine her virtue before letting myself get too excited. So as we spent time together with friends or on dates, I silently observed her conduct. Here is what I noticed:

- Ashley frequently invited a dejected girlfriend to join her for dinner and offered encouragement and wise counsel.
- While swing dancing with friends, Ashley asked the overlooked guys to dance with her.
- Ashley gave up several Saturday nights to help her mom clean the house for special parties.
- Ashley resolutely avoided sexual activity until marriage.
- Ashley went out of her way to welcome newcomers at church.

These were just a few of the situations that gave me insight into Ashley's character. Upon recognizing that this was her consistent style of behavior, I felt an assurance that Ashley understood the value of sacrificial love. This discovery encouraged my heart, but we still needed more time to determine our future.

As you discern someone's character, take your time and do not expect perfection. Everyone makes mistakes, slacks off, and acts selfishly on occasion. Be very careful, however, if a person's integrity appears erratic. Honesty, humility, and forgiveness should be normal traits, not rare ones. You want to date someone whose virtue is consistent.

You can also assess character by evaluating whether you feel safe with someone. As you spend time together, do you feel that he or she consistently is honest, sincere, and sensitive to your needs? This does not mean that virtue is boring or predictable. On the contrary, dating someone with good character should free you to have a blast together.

People with character take responsibility for their lives and don't blame others for their burdens. In contrast, people who refuse to admit their mistakes, handle their problems, or make their decisions still need to mature. They may live in a 35-year-old body, but their maturity level is that of a 15-year-old's. Adults remain trapped in adolescence when they want other people to do everything for them. Avoid romantic relationships with these types of people. You do not want to date a grown child.

Finally, be careful not to equate integrity with pious-looking behavior. Daily Bible reading, prayer, and volunteer work are all good, but they can be performed with prideful or selfish motives. Just because a Christian single looks righteous on the outside doesn't mean that his or her intentions are godly. Believers are capable of selfish behavior too, so do not think that dating a Christian automatically signifies that he or she has character. You still need to date him or her long enough to witness consistent, sacrificial behavior.

Christ, the Author of Sacrifice

If we are honest with ourselves, we must confess that a problem exists when we try to extend sacrificial love to another person; *We cannot consistently do it.* All of us possess some measure of loyalty, mercy, and self-control. Yet as conflict, disappointment, and everyday life set in, our desire to care for another person tends to disappear. If we are called on to sacrifice, we usually expect something in return or wait until the sacrifice becomes convenient for us.

However, sacrificial love is not about convenience or scratching each other's backs. Our romantic relationships are supposed to represent the way Christ gave Himself up for us (Ephesians 5:22-33). If we cannot love in this manner, what hope do we have? Only Jesus Christ has the power to offer sacrificial love regardless of the circumstance. He displayed the ultimate act of character by dying innocently upon a cross. In the same way, Jesus wants to live His integrity through us. Only by His power can we extend sacrificial love to another person—especially when we don't feel like it. All we have to do is yield our will to His. No fancy prayers are necessary; we simply invite Him by faith to live through us. In that moment, He takes over and imparts His character through our lives (Galatians 2:20).

Because of our inability to love sacrificially, the apostle Paul called love, joy, peace, patience, kindness, goodness, faithfulness, gentleness, and self-control the fruit of the Spirit (Galatians 5:22-23). Notice that they aren't called the fruit of human effort. Our relationships desperately need love, joy, peace, and kindness, but we cannot regularly treat others in that way. Therefore, Jesus urges us to rely upon Him as the Source of that behavior.

Too often, our human pride attempts to water down the fruit of the Spirit so that it will be easier for us to attain. For instance, in dating we tend to portray kindness as a woman planning a picnic for her new boyfriend. That is not necessarily real kindness. Christ's definition of kindness would involve the woman making a picnic for her boyfriend after an argument in which he hurt her feelings. She can choose to let Jesus love her boyfriend through her even when she doesn't feel like loving him.

Guys, you may think that sacrificial love is paying big money to take your girlfriend to a sold-out concert. That's a nice gesture, but Christ would define sacrifice as skipping the concert to talk out her frustrations after her awful day at work. (It may also mean not turning on the TV while she is talking.) To a guy, those actions may sound unreasonable or impractical. When you yield to Christ, however, He can give you the desire to change your plans, sit patiently with your girlfriend, and listen to her problems—and not just to score some bonus points.

True love means laying down your wishes to profit another person. Your spiritual union with Christ makes that kind of behavior possible. You can try to love in your own strength, but you will eventually burn out. Until you ask Jesus to live His sacrificial love through you, loving other people will always be a struggle. That is why He said, "With men this is impossible, but with God all things are possible" (Matthew 19:26).

In addition, as you apply this truth to your life, determine if the person you date seeks Christ for his or her source of sacrificial love. Take some time together to discuss whether he or she understands that Christ wants to live His life within us.

Character on Trial

We can also discover the character of a person by observing how he or she handles stress and trials. When the pressure mounts, does your date look for the easy way out? Is personal happiness so important that he or she breaks promises, passes blame, or ends the relationship? An individual who acts this way does not deserve your heart.

On the other hand, when someone continues to express love in the midst of difficult circumstances, you know his or her love is genuine.

> And not only this, but we also exult in our tribulations, knowing *that tribulation brings about perseverance; and perseverance, proven character;* and proven character, hope; and hope does not disappoint, because the love of God has been poured out within our hearts through the Holy Spirit who was given to us (Romans 5:3-5).

When someone is willing to love in the midst of tribulation, Christ can build character within that person. Tribulation is not necessarily a physical torture test. Rather, it is usually a moral battle within someone's mind and will. Faced with a frustrating circumstance, the person must act upon what he or she truly believes. The tribulation exposes the person's true convictions and desires.

Our sinful world guarantees plenty of tribulation. You do not need to discern your date's character by creating an ethical exam or asking a bunch of what-if questions. Instead, observe how he or she treats you when you are not getting along. Does he or she remain honest? Control his or her temper? Look for immediate gratification? Observe also how your date acts if he or she goes through bad circumstances, such as an illness, a job loss, or a money crunch. Does he or she blame God in anger or continue to depend on Christ? Singles who allow Jesus to live His sacrificial love through them in the midst of trials have the maturity necessary for a passionate marriage.

Seek the Total Package

When my friends ask me what to look for in a mate, I tell them to seek the "total package"—someone who attracts them physically, mentally, spiritually, and sacrificially. Ashley attracted me with plenty of outward attributes, but more importantly, she possessed the character that allowed me to trust her. Singles of this type are rare jewels, but they are worth the wait.

The best way to attract a "total package" is to become a "total package" yourself. Are you allowing Christ to make you desirable both in character and appearance? Are you willing to let Christ express His sacrificial love through you?

Wise singles know that beauty and charm will eventually fade away. Yet kindness, acceptance, and selflessness can keep a relationship passionate forever. Concentrate on the qualities that matter over time. *Your exterior may help others notice you, but your interior will help them celebrate you.*

Personal Bible Study

1. Read Matthew 7:15-21 and Galatians 6:7-9. What truth about discerning character in other people is mentioned in these verses?

2. What insight from Proverbs 22:3 can you apply when choosing whom to date?

3. List character qualities described in 1 Peter 3:1-7. Why are they important to relationships?

4. Read 1 Timothy 2:8-11 and 3:1-12. List the character qualities you should look for in a man or a woman.

5. Turn to 1 John 4:7-12 and reflect on the sacrificial love Jesus offered you. Consider three ways that you could love someone sacrificially in a dating relationship.

6. To begin listening to your heart, list the inward and outward characteristics that you most wish for in a mate. Pursue these desires that God has placed within you, and do not settle for less.

Group Discussion Questions

1. Discuss the attributes that attract you to the opposite sex the most, including physical, emotional, and spiritual characteristics.

2. What does specific attraction to the opposite sex parallel in your relationship with Christ?

3. Consider the list of reasons why relationships fail (page 64). Then name some reasons why your previous dating relationships ended. Did a lack of character or sacrificial love contribute to the breakup?

4. Discuss three ways that you can discern relational character in the person you date.

5. Identify three ways that sacrificial love could be exhibited in a dating relationship.

6. How can Christ's love for you protect you from choosing a bad dating partner?

The Pursuit of Passion

:: :: ::

Finding and Attracting Healthy Singles to Date

I was eating lunch with my friend Tom when he complained, "I want to date a mature, Christian woman, but I don't think there are any left."

I said, "I'm sure they exist, Tom. Have you considered that healthy, Christian women may be avoiding you?"

Surprised by my question, Tom replied, "Why would they avoid me? I'm a nice guy, and I treat women well."

"Tom, have you ever contemplated your reputation among the women in this town?" I asked. "Consider the last three girls you dated. Did they exhibit character or spiritual maturity? No, they acted ditzy and dressed seductively. When wise, Christian women see you dating these immature girls, they assume that you must also be relationally unhealthy. Thus, your reputation suffers, and the smart women keep their distance from you. That's why you can't find one."

Sometimes, the hardest part of building a passionate dating relationship is finding someone to date in the first place. I hear many singles gripe about how they rarely meet anyone attractive and godly. However, when I talk with these frustrated people, I discover that many of them are sabotaging their efforts. They deter the interest of the singles they want to meet through their poor reputation, negative demeanor, or immature relational skills.

This chapter will explore the two major factors that influence your ability to find and attract desirable singles. In the first section, we will expose some common relational problems that can undermine your attractiveness to the opposite sex. In the second section, we will discuss where to meet new singles and how to maximize your effectiveness. In addition, on pages 100–101, you will find a list of fun activities to try on those all-important first dates.

Obstacles That Inhibit Your Attractiveness

On a planet as big as ours, fun-loving, godly singles are everywhere. So if you are struggling to find the type of person your heart desires, you might consider whether you are part of the problem. Are you making yourself as appealing as possible to the kind of person you wish to date? If you want to go out with someone cute, intelligent, and mature, would that person consider you cute, intelligent, and mature?

People generally gravitate to those like them in attractiveness, character, and beliefs. Therefore, you might be looking for your soul mate in the right places but be ineffective at engaging them. To address this problem, let's look at five obstacles that can discourage people from wanting to date you, and then we will recognize how the love of Christ can remove these hindrances.

1. Poor Reputation

Have you heard the phrase "your reputation precedes you"? That statement may not sound fair, but your ability to attract mature singles can be spoiled if people regard you as superficial or immature.

Singles who have character generally reserve their affections for other singles with character. In this chapter's opening story, my friend Tom never considered the possibility that single women might have a bad opinion of him. Yet I had talked with a few of the girls whom Tom wished to date and learned that his behavior turned them off. They had watched him date several immature women and lost respect for him. The quality of your friends and your past relationships can definitely affect your dating prospects.

Does this mean that you should constantly worry about the opinions of other people? No. Humans are fickle, and you will go crazy if you try to please everyone. Instead, realize that singles decide whom they date based on outward appearances and reputation. Smart singles keep their eyes open for those who display character. When they see them, they approach those individuals and start friendships. Therefore, if you do not exhibit character, you may be driving mature singles away from you.

To examine your reputation, ask yourself, *Do I allow Christ to live His patience, honesty, and humility through me?* In addition, when Jesus urges you to consider the needs of others, do you follow those promptings, or do you concentrate on yourself? Pure passion allows Christ to live His sacrificial love through you, and that determines not only your character but also how others view you.

Your reputation can suffer when you pursue desires simply to gratify yourself. For instance, if you date just for sex, demand the attention of others, or regularly groan about your problems, people will consider you immature. Your attractiveness to wise singles will diminish. So if you struggle to meet the kind of person your heart prefers, take a look at yourself.

Should you discover that your character is a hindrance to your dating prospects, don't try to be straightlaced to impress people. A phony reputation is worse than a bad one. Instead, ask Christ to improve your character by living His life through you. Your social standing will not improve overnight, but as you respond to His prompting to be honest, patient, and authentic, people around you will take notice.

2. Negative Demeanor

Sandy was a beautiful young woman, but her beauty faded after her relationship with Ron ended. A year later, her face still reflected the disappointment and frustration of the breakup. Unbeknownst to Sandy, several men had hoped to date her when they heard that she was available. However, when they saw the bitterness on her face, they quickly lost interest.

A person's demeanor reflects his or her attitudes and thoughts. Accordingly, some singles who have experienced rejection, abuse, or failure still wear the pain on their faces. They look pessimistic or unapproachable. Frankly, this is a turnoff because no one relishes dating someone who seems callous or despondent. Life is hard enough without having to deal with a constantly negative person. For that reason, most people prefer to spend time with someone who is cheerful or helps make life a little more enjoyable.

A happy demeanor attracts people because when you smile, you welcome people into your life. This is why smiling men and women naturally appear more attractive and inviting. A smile helps other people lower their guard and become more sociable.

Why do some singles rarely smile? The problem stems from an insecure or negative self-esteem. If people feel inferior or uncomfortable with themselves, their faces can reflect it. A smile is hard to fake, and a cheerful countenance cannot be fabricated. Instead, a real change has to take place within.

If you have difficulty smiling or enjoying humor, your negative demeanor can deter other singles from socializing with you. How can you change your countenance? Lasting change can occur when you allow the truth of Christ's unconditional love to liberate you from pleasing others (John 8:32). By resting in His acceptance, your past mistakes or the opinions of your peers no longer determine your self-esteem. You are free to view life from the Lord's point of view, and He is always positive. Even during your trials, Jesus is excited about the good that will result. This does not imply that you should ignore your grief or hardships. You should accept and deal with tragedy in your life, but remember that Christ always has a positive outlook on your life. To transform a negative demeanor, start by reviewing your spiritual wedding gifts listed in chapter 2.

3. Poor Relational Skills

A third deterrent to attracting desirable singles is a poorly developed set of relational skills. Generally, people avoid spending time with those who are self-absorbed, babble incessantly, or are too shy to talk. We've all experienced the strain of socializing with a person who either dominates a discussion or makes you carry the conversation.

Sadly, many singles never receive relational instruction or develop proper social skills. This does not mean, however, that inappropriate behavior has to continue. Anyone can take steps to improve his or her relational manners.

The first step toward growth is to honestly assess how you relate to others. Ask yourself the following questions:

- When I talk to people, does the conversation usually revolve around me?
- Do I allow other people to state their opinions in a discussion?
- Do I forget to ask questions about the other person during a conversation?
- Do I sit shyly and make other people do most of the talking?
- Do I have trouble looking at someone when he or she is talking to me?

If you answered yes to any of these questions or were unsure, your relational skills could be a barrier to your dating life. Before moving on, examine another set of questions:

- Do I know how to show interest in the subjects other people talk about?
- Do I consistently exhibit consideration and respect for the opposite sex?
- Do I know how to read nonverbal cues and end a conversation?

- Do I know how to discover what makes another person feel special?
- When I know what makes a person feel special, do I frequently express it?

If you answered no to any of these questions, you may need to cultivate better relational skills. Plenty of resources are available to help you improve how you relate to others. You can read books on interpersonal communication, ask a close friend to make you aware of annoying habits, take classes in social skills, or discuss your situation with a Christian counselor.

When you socialize with people, you have the choice to either love them or use them to meet your needs. Immature behavior could indicate a dependence on others to validate your self-esteem or make you happy. You cannot build good relationships if you neglect the needs of others.

For example, I have a bad habit of chatting with friends and forgetting to ask them anything about their lives. I tend to babble about myself during the entire conversation. To improve how I relate with people, I have asked Christ to prompt my heart when I forget to concentrate on others. Since then, on several occasions I have felt His desire within me to pay better attention to someone else's concerns.

As you discover your relational tendencies, invite Christ to make you more sensitive to the ways that you interact with others. In addition, consider the interests, wishes, and feelings of others as more important than your own (Philippians 2:3). As you learn to relate in love, you will make yourself a better candidate for a dating relationship.

4. Fear of Rejection

When I graduated from college, I joined a bachelor's Bible study at my church. We met once a week to pray and study Scripture. Our discussions, however, regularly gravitated to the subject of dating. We sat around bragging about the girls we thought had crushes on us. We even developed individual lists of women whom we considered our "dating all-stars." Any woman who made our number one spot earned the title of "franchise player," which meant we hoped to sign her to a lifetime contract (ladies, that's sports talk for marriage). As you can tell, we were not role models for maturity. We talked a lot about dating but rarely did much about it. That's because most of us were either too fearful of rejection or too clueless to effectively ask a girl out.

You cannot blame a dull dating life on a lack of attractive singles if you are too afraid to get involved. If you want to date, you have to get out and meet people. This goes for women as well as men. You will not progress if you are too scared to open up and interact. A fear of rejection will only keep you in a relational rut. To stimulate your social life, look for ways to get involved with other singles and make yourself available.

Rejection in dating is unavoidable because you cannot please everyone. Therefore, expect some disappointment and remember that the success of your dating life does not determine your identity. Your primary need for love is already met in Jesus Christ, and dating relationships are secondary. Jesus says that He unconditionally accepts you even if others reject you. Believe me, He understands rejection because He endured the rejection of the whole world (Luke 23:20-25). This is why Christ's love can help you overcome your anxiety about failure. Jesus replaces your fear of rejection with the assurance that His passion for you will never change. Let's examine how Christ's love can influence the way that you initiate a date.

Tips for Guys When Asking Out a Woman

Guys, I know the feelings of nervousness when asking a woman for a date. I used to stare at the phone, terrified that my voice would crack or that I would run out of things to say. Eventually, though, I had to put aside my fear and take action. Below are a few suggestions that helped me start:

1. First, ask yourself if the woman you want to date has a definite interest in you. For instance, have you had a pleasant conversation with her that lasted for more than a minute? If not, or if you are unclear about her interest level, you might want to take more time to get to know her. Otherwise, you could come across as pushy.

2. Before you ask a woman out, determine what you might share in common, such as hobbies, church, or mutual friends. Use this information to help break the ice when you call her.

3. Plan the activities for a date before you ask a woman out. Women appreciate guys who put some thought and creativity into their time together. See pages 100–101 for a list of ideas.

4. At least four days before you want to get together, call her or ask her for a date in person. Do not leave a phone message or send an e-mail because if you don't hear back from her, you won't know if she is ignoring you or if she never got your message. If you can't reach her after two or three phone attempts, wait patiently until you can ask her in person. (You will look desperate if you show up too frequently on her caller ID.)

5. If she says no to your offer, tell her that's fine and leave her alone. Your self-esteem is not based on her approval of you. Jesus loves you regardless of her answer.

6. If she says yes, pick her up on time, have fun, and act as a gentleman would (open doors for her, compliment her, and pay for everything). Also, don't rush to judgment about your future together. Months will pass before you really know her.

Tips for Ladies to Get a Guy Interested in You

Ladies, maybe you wonder if asking a man out on a date is prudent. I believe that you are free to try, but I would advise against it for two reasons. First, assertive women are a turnoff to most men. Second, men need to learn how to lead in relationships. If a guy won't lead in the beginning of a relationship, then he likely will not do so later. If you know a guy whom you wish to date, wait until he asks you out. I know that waiting for a man to call you can be agonizing, but it is worth it in the long run.

However, you do not have to wait passively. If you meet a man who interests your heart, you can do some things to increase the chances that he will call you:

1. When you are around a man whom you like, strike up a conversation with him and attempt to determine his interest in you. As you talk, honestly ask yourself, "Does he truly seem attracted to me?" Generally, you can tell by whether or not he keeps his attention on you.

2. Get involved in some of the same group activities in which the guy you like participates, such as volunteer groups, recreational teams, and Bible studies. This will increase your exposure to him and your chances to talk. However, don't fake an interest in the activities. Get involved out of a genuine desire.

3. Plan a group activity and invite the guy you like. You can throw a party, have people over for dinner, arrange for a group to go dancing, attend a concert, or watch a sporting event. (Ladies, this tip really works. Ashley used it on me when I was nervous about asking her out.)

4. If you try these methods and the man fails to show an interest in you, then forget him and move on with your life. He was not your only chance at a passionate relationship. Rest in Christ's love for you and wait to attract another man.

5. When a man does ask you out, clarify his plans. For safety reasons, avoid first-date activities in which you will be alone together. Instead, do something in a public

place. See pages 100–101 for a helpful list of ideas. Also, if you are uncertain about a guy's intentions, you might want to meet him for lunch first. Above all, do not give your heart to a man until you have determined his character.

6. Finally, do not be afraid of dating rejection because you believe that you have nothing to offer someone. If you are depressed or focused on yourself, then you probably don't have much to contribute. However, when you possess integrity and the love of Jesus Christ, you definitely have something to offer another person. You don't need the most attractive face, the best body, or the most money to be interesting to the opposite sex. Those things are fine, but they do not hold relationships together. Your character and Christ living within you make you worth getting to know.

5. Lack of Appeal

Beauty is in the eye of the beholder. If you do not understand what beauty means to the opposite sex, they might regard you as unappealing. You can impair your dating life if you do not know how to make yourself attractive to the kind of person you want to date. For example, if you hope to date a model, are you attempting to make yourself equally as striking? Or if you want to date someone outgoing and popular, are you also well-known?

If you have trouble getting a date, you may be unaware of what the opposite sex appreciates. Start by asking a trusted friend of that gender for advice on how to improve your appearance. Could you use a makeover or an updated wardrobe? Could you better accentuate your physical assets? Nothing is unspiritual about increasing your allure to other singles.

You don't need to focus solely on your body to attract the opposite sex. Updating your hairstyle or losing weight can certainly help, but many nonphysical changes can make you more charming. For instance, some women could improve their appeal if they were more feminine, smiled more often, or carried themselves with confidence. Likewise, some men would be a better catch if they were not so macho or self-absorbed. Be honest with yourself and look for ways to become more interesting.

You can also diminish your attractiveness if you are one-dimensional. This means that others consider you boring because you have a limited number of interests or hobbies. If you are not well-rounded, others may have difficulty connecting with you because you have little to talk about or enjoy together. You may need to get involved with popular activities so that you can relate better to people. In addition, consider broadening your range of skills or interests. Pursue new hobbies that fascinate you. Taking steps such as these can enhance your ability to attract mature singles.

Once you discover what appeals to the opposite sex, you will be faced with the question, am I willing to do what is necessary to make myself more attractive? If not, then a big reason why you can't find a date is yourself. Human love is conditional, so people will rarely accept you just as you are. Thus, part of life on this planet involves pleasing people. In the process, you should not sell out to superficiality. Character is more important. However, taking steps to improve your appeal reveals your ability to sacrifice for another person's benefit. This kind of selflessness helps to initiate and sustain a passionate relationship.

Finally, be realistic in your expectations of who might find you appealing, but don't sell yourself short. Pursue someone who captivates your heart. If he or she rejects you for superficial reasons consider it a blessing. That person did you a favor by exposing his or her immaturity before you got deeply involved. Mature Christian singles do not focus entirely upon physical attributes. They appreciate beauty but desire integrity more.

Where the Singles Are

In this second section, we will examine the pros and cons of the most common ways to meet singles. Keep in mind, however, that no one proven way exists to find a good person to date. The key is to use all of the options at your disposal.

1. The Church

The local church is an excellent place to meet attractive, mature, Christian singles. It is one of the few locations where singles with possibly the same beliefs and interests as yours regularly gather. Essentially, all you have to do is show up, become involved, and get to know people. A large church can be especially helpful if it has a singles ministry. If you attend a church that doesn't have a singles group, ask whether it has other activities, such as singles Bible studies, monthly socials, or retreats.

The large size of some church congregations might seem intimidating. Therefore, you may feel inclined to visit just the worship service and then go home. However, you limit your opportunity to meet singles if you take such a narrow approach. The best way to break into a large singles group is to get involved in their activities. Most churches have sports teams, music programs, or mission trips that offer great ways to meet new people. Find somewhere to serve short-term so that you can get exposure to people. Offer to volunteer for something that interests you, such as teaching, organizing parties, working with youth, or opening your home for Bible studies. By participating, you get to serve the church body with your time as well as improve your chances of meeting other singles.

If the singles group at your present church becomes stagnant, visit another church. You can do this without withdrawing from your current church. Simply find a friend to join you one or two Sundays a month to investigate other churches in your area. You could also visit another church during its Sunday evening or weeknight services. This allows you to stay involved at your home church while broadening your association with other Christians.

Meeting singles at a church can be fruitful, but remember this caution: Church congregations are comprised of people at various maturity levels. Church attendance does not prove that a person is a Christian. Furthermore, professing to be a Christian does not guarantee relational maturity or a willingness to love sacrificially.

The church is not a dating haven. Many singles with bad intentions purposely hide out in Christian groups to take advantage of the unsuspecting (Romans 16:17-18). They usually target young singles who are unaware of their schemes. Stalking and date rape have occurred within many church groups. Keep your judgment sharp, and do not trust someone until you have determined his or her character.

Regardless of the bad apples, the church is still one of the best places to meet healthy singles who are passionate about sharing the love of Christ. Take advantage of the available fellowship to benefit yourself as well as those you meet.

2. Recommendations from Friends and Family

Friends and family can be another good source to help you find mature singles. However, they cannot recommend attractive candidates unless you specifically tell them what type of person you desire to date. Give them more information than "I want to date someone cute." Honestly define what you desire regarding such characteristics as outward appearances, interests, education level, and spiritual background. As we discussed in the previous chapter, you do not want to settle for just anybody. You want to find someone who completely captivates your heart.

Also, be open to alternate suggestions from family and friends. Consider their recommendations if they can clearly explain why their candidate is worth meeting. On the other hand, be wary of well-meaning relatives who simply want to get you married. If they lack discretion, they may waste your time by setting you up with anyone who comes to mind. Thank them kindly and say no.

Above all, make sure that your friends and family understand the importance of character. If they cannot confirm a potential date's maturity, then they aren't doing you any favors. You do not want to walk into a date blindly. Ask your friends to find out more specifics about someone's integrity before they refer him or her to you. If they can introduce you to someone they know is mature, then thank them and go out on the date but continue to guard your heart until you get to know that individual yourself.

3. Organizations That Match Your Interests

Singles who are exploring opportunities to meet other singles commonly overlook organizations that match their beliefs and interests. These can include colleges or any other institutions where you continue your education. Besides school, however, you can participate in such groups as nondenominational Bible studies, youth or inner-city ministries, and nonprofit organizations.

Other options include organizations that deal with your favorite interests, such as a sports team, a business association, a community service program, or a drama troupe. When you interact with someone who shares your interests, you already have a foundation on which to build a relationship. In addition, you get to enjoy new people in a comfortable environment. Moreover, large organizations offer great opportunities for meeting people because they usually have a constant cycle of newcomers. This can increase your exposure to many more individuals.

Just as with churches, though, do not assume that the people you meet are Christians or relationally mature. Take your time getting to know people and stay focused on finding a person whose character attracts you.

Finally, out of respect for these organizations, do not join a group just to meet people. Participate out of a genuine interest. That way, you do not waste the organization's time by quickly losing interest and deciding to leave.

4. Dating Services

Dating services are popping up everywhere, especially on the Internet. These companies let you search for singles who meet your list of desired characteristics or match you to someone in their database. You can look at a person's picture, read their profile, and even send quirky questions for them to answer. Other services offer features such as compatibility testing or video footage of a candidate in action. Dating services offer a modern way to meet new people, but they have several drawbacks to consider.

First, dating services cannot discern someone's character for you—that is your responsibility. A dating service may locate someone for you who has blond hair and likes sushi, but it cannot confirm that the individual is spiritually mature or desires to love sacrificially.

Unfortunately, too many singles lower their guard once a dating service says they've found them a match. They get emotionally excited, assume that the dating service computer must be right, and rush into a relationship before they verify the other person's integrity over time. The problem stems from shameless marketing tactics by dating services that promise success and our own desire to speed up the dating process. We want results as soon as possible, and dating services, whether online or off, advertise the fast track to romance. Ironically, statistics reveal that less than one percent of dating service subscribers actually find a marriage partner that way![1]

Second, dating services hinder people's ability to be themselves. When singles use a dating service, they are under scrutiny, so they put on their best faces. This is normal, but it prevents you from learning the truth about people. Be extra cautious if you choose to go out with someone through a dating service. Meet candidates in public places when you first get together. Keep your personal information private, such as home address, phone numbers, and office location. Use e-mail or the dating service administrator to coordinate your communication.

Finally, be aware of the high-priced fees and shaky credibility of some dating services. Ask for referrals to verify that a service is legitimate. Dating is expensive enough without hiring someone to help you. Thus, I recommend using the free methods first to find Christian singles.

5. Singles Hangouts

Singles hangouts, such as bars, beaches, and dance clubs can be scary places to meet new people. While they might offer a lot of fun, they also contain an element of danger, especially for women. If you decide to go out dancing or enjoy a day at the beach, it is best to go with trusted friends.

Remember that most people you encounter at bars and beaches may not have your best intentions in mind. Those fleshly environments encourage people to interact selfishly. Also, discerning a person's character can be difficult when he or she is in a dim, smoky room or sunning half-naked in the sand. Therefore, I consider these places detrimental for finding mature singles.

I am not suggesting that you avoid beaches or nightclubs. Just don't expect to meet many mature Christian singles at those locations. They may be there, but they will have their guard up. Finally, be prepared to leave immediately if someone approaches you in a lustful or disrespectful manner.

6. The Internet and Long-Distance Relationships

With the advent of the Internet, some singles now spend hours trying to develop intimacy with someone via a plastic box. E-mail and Internet chat rooms allow you to communicate with a normal person one day and a serial killer the next. That's what makes these online methods so dangerous—you never truly know who someone is.

The bottom line is that nothing can replace face-to-face communication. A physical separation allows someone to fake his or her true feelings and intentions. Likewise, discerning someone's character is almost impossible unless you spend time together. Thus, I urge you to avoid dating over the Internet and divulging your personal information to strangers. Otherwise, you make yourself vulnerable to relational wolves.

Can you make a long-distance dating relationship work? Possibly, but you will have to put forth a huge effort to truly get to know someone. Long-distance relationships benefit you little until you decide to spend major amounts of time together. You can learn about a person's interests and beliefs over a fiber-optic cable, but you cannot discern if he or she has character unless you are in the same place.

Talk is cheap when discerning integrity, and so are letters and e-mails. You need to be able to observe consistent actions of maturity before you can trust someone with your heart. I don't mean to sound harsh, but you might be desperate if you are willing to undertake a long-distance relationship with someone you've just met. Instead, focus on some of the other methods we have already discussed and find someone that you can date locally.

The Best Way to Meet Singles: Live with Passion

In my opinion, the best way to meet mature singles is to follow the desires that Christ puts within your heart. The Christian life is not about dating, careers, or getting married. The Christian life is about living in union with a Person—Jesus Christ.

Jesus gives you desires to explore new interests and meet new people (Ephesians 2:10). How do you recognize His desires? Start by asking yourself, *What have I always wanted to do? Where have I always wanted to go?* Christ doesn't give ideas that are boring, abstract, or irresponsible. Following your heart means pursuing something that truly makes you passionate. It could be starting a new business, exploring a new hobby, traveling to a new place, attending a new church, or moving to a new location. Like me, you might even desire to write a book!

People respect those who follow their dreams. Therefore, if you pursue the aspirations that Christ puts in your heart, you can become more attractive to others. In addition, you may meet someone who shares your passion, and suddenly you have a new friend.

We all want to live the abundant life that Christ spoke about in John 10:10. Yet He said that this abundant life would only occur as we let Him live it through us (John 15:4-7). He has a wonderful adventure planned for you. It may involve living in a small, quiet town, or it may take you around the world. Regardless of what His plan looks like, it will fulfill you.

To explore your internal urgings from Jesus, consider what is the passion of your heart. If you are unsure, take a small step of faith and try something. You might begin by volunteering somewhere, taking a class, or signing up for a short-term mission trip. Expose yourself to the things that you really want to do.

Jesus is your true Husband and Provider, and part of His provision is to lead you into new relationships. So pursue the passion that Christ puts within your heart. You never know who you might meet.

Great First-Date Activities

A fun way to start a dating relationship is to learn a new hobby together. It helps foster communication and creates respect. Here are some great first-date ideas that you can try together:

- Take a dance lesson: swing, salsa, ballroom.
- Take a sports lesson: tennis, golf, rock climbing, kayaking.
- Take an art class: painting, sketching, pottery. (Some cities have art cafés in which you can paint or work with pottery while you enjoy a meal together.)

Your first date should consist of an activity that stimulates conversation. Here are several ideas to help you keep the discussion flowing:

- Visit an art gallery.
- Visit a botanical garden.
- Visit an amusement park.
- Visit the zoo (a proven winner).
- Visit a state park or nature center.
- Visit a history, art, or science museum.

- Visit a church service or Bible study and go for coffee afterward.
- Play board games together.
- Go horseback riding.
- Go ice skating.
- Go whitewater rafting with a group.
- Go to a coffee shop or a dessert café.
- Go inline skating or bicycling at a local park.
- Go on a picnic (girls, make sure it's in a public place).
- Go to a sporting event.

Some first-date activities prevent good conversation or prematurely encourage physical activity. Here are some activities you might want to avoid on your first date:

- concerts (too loud to talk)
- movies (no chance to talk)
- the theater (too quiet to talk)
- comedy clubs (trashy, sexual language)
- loud restaurants or sports bars (too distracting to talk)
- renting a movie (risk of getting physical prematurely)
- a picnic in a secluded area (risk of physical danger)

Personal Bible Study

1. Reflect upon Philippians 2:3-8. Do you consider the needs of others when you talk to them? Do you do anything that people find annoying? Ask God to point out any self-centered attitudes.

2. Read Proverbs 13:3 and 18:6-7,12, and consider why the quality of your relational skills affects your social life.

3. In Luke 23:20-25, Jesus was rejected though He was innocent. You are united with Christ. How can He strengthen you against the fear of dating rejection?

4. From Romans 16:17-18, what warning could be suggested about meeting singles to date at your church? What three caution signs are you advised to look for when assessing someone's character?

5. What discouragement does 1 John 3:18 imply about dating via e-mail, telephone, or Internet chat rooms?

6. Ephesians 2:10 and Philippians 2:13 state that God puts desires within you to try new activities and meet new people. List two desires that you feel within your heart right now. How might pursuing these desires invigorate your social life?

Group Discussion Questions

1. Talk about why a good reputation is important for attracting other singles with character.

2. Discuss some misconceptions concerning the things that attract men and women. For example, macho attitudes generally turn off women. Based on what is said, consider if you need to change how you make yourself attractive to the opposite sex.

3. Consider the drawbacks of going on a blind date without first obtaining a character reference.

4. List three good places to meet mature singles in your area.

5. Talk about the physical and relational dangers of trying to meet mature singles at the typical singles hangouts.

6. Consider the reasons why living passionately makes you more attractive to other singles.

6

THE ENEMY
OF PASSION

:: :: ::

The Impact of Sin on Your Dating Life

Chuck fought the desire to lash out at his girlfriend, Leah. While shopping at the mall, they had bumped into her ex-boyfriend, Dan. A quick hello turned into a conversation that Leah seemed to enjoy. Chuck was a Christian and knew that he should be considerate. Nevertheless, the more he listened to Leah laugh with Dan, the more a jealous anger brewed within him.

The interaction made Chuck worry. *I thought that Leah liked me, but maybe she wants to date Dan again,* he said to himself. His fear and jealousy suddenly reached the boiling point. He grabbed Leah's arm and announced, "Time's up, Leah. Let's go!" He pulled her away from Dan in a show of force, but it backfired.

"Let go of me, Chuck! How could you be so rude?" she exclaimed.

"We need to get going," Chuck urged.

"Well, if you are in such a hurry, then leave," Leah replied. "I'll have Dan drive me home!"

Chuck couldn't believe his stupid outburst. He wished he could crawl into a hole and disappear.

You would think that if Christian singles wanted to share God's love together, then all of their relationships would be godly and loving. Yet we all know that reality can be quite a different experience. Christians can act just as sinfully as non-Christians can.

Do you find that sin regularly spoils your relationships? Do you wonder whether Christianity even has any benefit to your dating life? Does a healthy dating relationship seem beyond your reach? I wrestled with these questions until I recognized the deception of sin and the freedom that Christ makes available. In this chapter we will expose sin's trickery, reveal your victory in Christ, and apply it to your dating life.

You Are Not Your Enemy

Do you know why sinful urges can feel so strong within you? In Chuck's case, he knew he should remain patient with Leah. But so much anger welled up inside him that he blew his temper— all while standing in a shopping mall. What caused his sudden outburst?

Unfortunately, many Christians are taught that responses like Chuck's are the results of a sinful nature. This common fallacy is promoted by people who believe that Christians have two natures warring against one another. They say that one part of you is holy and fights to do good. Meanwhile, another part of you is sinful and desires to do evil. For good behavior to occur, you must strengthen your good side as much as possible.

This dual-nature theory presents evil behavior as a natural, irrepressible part of you. It classifies sin as something you do by nature. Therefore, yielding to your evil desires is inevitable because you naturally want to do it. This theory offers no hope against overcoming temptation. Worse, it prompts the question, if God is holy, how could He love and dwell within an evil person such as me?

Instead, the Bible clearly states that Christians have only one, holy nature. When you accepted Jesus as your Lord and Savior,

THE ENEMY OF PASSION

God says He removed your old sin nature and exchanged it with the holy nature of Christ. Because this truth is so significant to your dating life, let's take a moment to understand the change that God performed within you.

One Nature Under God

Every human is born with a natural bent toward selfishness. This innate tendency is called the sinful nature, and it is the result of Adam and Eve's sin in the Garden of Eden (Romans 5:12). The evil that they committed was passed on to all of us. You may notice it when you are around a child who has hit the "terrible twos." What was born as mom's bundle of joy is now a pouting, temper-tantrum-throwing, self-seeking little person. The child's parents didn't have to teach the kid how to misbehave. All boys and girls know how to sin on their own.

Before you became a Christian, you possessed a sinful nature, which suppressed the motivation to act virtuously. Sinning came naturally to you. For example, when you faced a decision to be compassionate or selfish, I doubt you had to struggle to justify a selfish decision. You simply did whatever you wanted to do. Under the control of sin, you had little desire to live for God or the benefit of others. However, when you accepted Jesus into your heart, God removed sin's control over you by crucifying your old, sinful nature and replacing it with the holy nature of Christ:

> Knowing this, that *our old self was crucified with Him*, in order that our body of sin might be done away with, that we should no longer be slaves to sin; for *he who has died is freed from sin*. Now if we have died with Christ, we believe that we shall also live with Him (Romans 6:6-8).

> Therefore if anyone is in Christ, he is a new creature; *the old things passed away; behold, new things have come....* He made Him who knew no sin to be sin on our behalf,

so that we might become the righteousness of God in
Him (2 Corinthians 5:17,21).

Once you became a Christian, you became a new creation.
Your old, sinful nature was eliminated, and the righteous nature
of Christ comprises your new identity. This is significant because
it confirms that you are no longer evil. You are not engaged in a
civil war—a sinful nature fighting against a holy nature. Instead,
your faith in the death and resurrection of Christ has made you
100 percent righteous in God's eyes.

Why Are You Tempted?

As a Christian, you are no longer in bondage to sin. You may
not believe it, however, when you harbor jealous, demanding, or
angry thoughts. Remember Chuck's episode at the mall? Though
God removed his sinful nature, Chuck still felt jealousy and
unrighteous anger. Why did bad behavior appeal to Chuck, who
is a Christian? The apostle Paul says that indwelling sin instigated
his evil desires:

> For the good that I want, I do not do; but I practice the
> very evil that I do not want. But if I am doing the very
> thing I do not want, *I am no longer the one doing it, but
> sin which dwells in me.* I find then the principle that *evil
> is present in me, the one who wants to do good* (Romans
> 7:19-21).

Paul clearly states in these verses that he did not create his
desire to do evil. Instead, he wanted to do good. Yet a separate
entity of sin was present within Paul's body, urging him to do evil.
Notice in verse 20 that Paul says, "I am no longer the one doing
it, but sin which dwells in me." The word "sin" in this verse is a
noun. In fact, Paul uses "sin" as a noun 40 times in the book of
Romans.[1] He claims that his desire for evil did not come from
him. If evil was his true desire, then he wouldn't feel guilty or wish

that he would do good. Therefore, an independent source within Paul's body generated his impulse to sin:

> For while we were in the flesh, the sinful passions, which were aroused by the Law, were at work in the members of our body to bear fruit for death (Romans 7:5).

When God removed your sinful nature, He ended sin's domination over your spirit, which defines who you are. However, sin still remains within your *body*. That is why you get sick, feel weary, and experience the allure of temptation. Sin infects your body like a foreign virus.

Indwelling sin can also influence your mind like a radio lodged within you that broadcasts tempting programs. For instance, when a man faces the decision to lie to his girlfriend, indwelling sin subtly promotes the urge within him to be dishonest. Because of the man's free will, he can choose whether to follow this unholy influence or act with integrity. In another example, suppose a woman bumps into her ex-boyfriend. Sin in her body acts as a radio, broadcasting the mental idea to boast about her new boyfriend. In her free will, she chooses whether to believe and yield to this temptation. In both cases, the man and the woman did not instigate their evil desires—sin residing in their bodies caused the problem.

Satan uses indwelling sin to arouse the thought that you would be happier if you pursued selfish desires rather than trusting in Christ. Again, you don't come up with the idea to be evil, because you are holy. All temptations originate from Satan's usage of indwelling sin to trash-talk your mind and body. Temptation by itself, however, is not sin. You fall into sin only when you choose to act upon a temptation. Do not beat yourself up or call yourself a bad person. In Christ, you are a righteous person who has the choice to follow sin's enticements (Colossians 1:21-23).

Why does God let sin dwell within a Christian's body? Sin remains within us for two reasons. The first is so that we can keep our free will. Remember from our discussion in chapter 3 that

God gave us a free will so we could experience true love with Him. Love is not love without a choice. That's why God allowed Adam and Eve to be tempted in the Garden of Eden (Genesis 3:1-7). If humans could not be tempted, we would all be like robots and incapable of intimate relationships.

Second, God does not remove sin from your body because your earthly body is destined to perish (1 Corinthians 15:35-50). Worn out bodies of skin, bones, and blood have no place in heaven. God is a Spirit and identifies you by your spirit and soul. Therefore, when you die, your body stays behind. Your soul and spirit, however, live on eternally with Christ. At the resurrection of the dead, you will receive a glorified body, free from sin (1 Corinthians 15:42-44). Imagine how wonderful that will be— no more acne or bad hair days!

Living in the Flesh

Until you die, you will walk the earth with a body that contains sin. Yet, the real purpose of sin is not to make you act as immorally as possible. Instead, Satan wants to convince you that Christ's love has no benefit for your life. He originates his deception by encouraging you to prefer something tangible to satisfy you, such as a girlfriend, a boyfriend, marriage, money—anything but Jesus. Whenever you decide to pursue something other than Christ for your fulfillment, you live in sinful self-sufficiency, apart from God. The Bible calls this independent mind-set "the flesh."

> For the flesh sets its desire against the Spirit, and the Spirit against flesh; for these things are in opposition to one another, so that you may not do the things that you please.... Now those who belong to Christ Jesus have crucified the flesh with its passion and desires (Galatians 5:17,24).

Basically, the flesh is a condition in which a person operates out of his or her own resources, doing things his or her own way.[2] It all started before you became a Christian, when you developed certain methods of finding happiness or success in life apart from God. You may have developed habits such as anger, alcoholism, promiscuity, timidity, pleasing people, or working too much. How the particular behavior looks on the surface doesn't matter. God considers fleshly activity anything that you do with a self-reliant motive (Proverbs 16:2; Romans 14:23).

When you became a Christian, God made you holy and righteous, but He did not erase your self-centered habits. So as you move through life, you still carry tendencies to control people and circumstances. These habits remain stored in your brain as selfish manipulation techniques or "flesh patterns." Whenever you decide to walk independently of Christ, your flesh patterns can be revived on a moment's notice. For instance, if a woman learned as a child to gain what she wanted by throwing tantrums, indwelling sin recalls that flesh pattern to tempt her to control her boyfriend with anger.

The flesh continuously rules a non-Christian's dating life because he or she is governed by the sinful nature. In a Christian, however, the flesh sabotages a dating relationship whenever a person chooses not to walk by faith in Christ. Furthermore, the flesh can influence people to date for selfish reasons and yet appear loving on the surface. For example, the flesh will urge a man to buy his girlfriend flowers, open the car door for her, and give her a compliment—just to get sex from her. On the other hand, if that man walks by faith in Christ, he will feel led to do those things out of humility and sacrifice. Your motives, not your actions, determine fleshly behavior.

Two Types of Flesh

Sinful temptations in relationships are not limited to extreme urges for sex, money, or control. Indwelling sin might use one of two types of flesh patterns to control you: positive flesh or negative flesh. Positive flesh tries to lure you into sin by reasoning that you are proficient enough to manage your life apart from God. By contrast, negative flesh attempts to persuade you that life is so hard that you need something other than God to get through it. Let's examine the subtlety of positive flesh first.

If you have experienced achievements or worldly success, sin may entice you with an attitude of pride. Because of your pattern of competence, you may think, *I am a good person. Everyone likes me,* or *God should be glad to have me on His team.* This is sin's attempt to convince you to reject God by appealing to you in a "positive" way.

You can succumb to this narcissistic deception if you consider yourself self-assured, self-righteous, dominant, deserving, or faultless. Essentially, you don't think you need God's help because you believe that you can handle life on your own. Therefore, walking by faith in Christ seems unnecessary.

Positive flesh denies that a Christian's true success only comes from God (2 Corinthians 3:5). But the Lord disregards any successful action that you perform in pride. In addition, when you live in overconfidence, you usually resist relying upon Christ until your circumstances get out of control. You see God as a safety net rather than your source for life.

Positive flesh also harms your dating relationships by making you self-centered or overly critical of anyone who does not meet your flawless standards. For example, I know a man with positive flesh who holds women to such high standards that his relationships never last. No woman seems good enough for him. Likewise, I know a woman who tends to view dating as a game of conquering a man's heart. She dates long enough to get a guy interested in her. Then, once she wins his affection, she breaks up and moves on to date someone else. Sometimes, she even goes out with a guy she doesn't care about just to show how popular she is.

If you notice a similar self-centered attitude within you, realize that indwelling sin is using a positive flesh pattern to mislead you. Love cannot coexist with pride, so you will have a hard time forming intimate relationships if you believe that you are God's gift to the world.

On the other hand, Satan can also bother you with negative flesh patterns, which make you feel worthless. If you have a history of pain, rejection, or abuse, Satan will use negative flesh to magnify your attitude of inferiority by persecuting you with thoughts of anxiety, insignificance, self-condemnation, helplessness, or self-pity. He utilizes the flesh to assert that only human affection can satisfy your heart. If you buy his lie, you can develop a craving for the opposite sex to accept you.

Personally, I struggle with negative flesh patterns that turned my dating relationships into a desperate pursuit to find security and boost my low self-esteem. I became so frantic that I rationalized dating immature women just to say I had a girlfriend. When my relationships failed, negative flesh tormented me with thoughts of worry, cynicism, or depression. It was Satan's ploy to make me feel as hopeless as possible.

The type of flesh that you struggle against is usually formed by circumstances in your childhood and teenage years. Yet you can wrestle with both positive and negative flesh throughout your life. Knowing the kind of flesh that you are vulnerable to helps you more easily spot Satan's lies and eliminate them with the love of Christ. For instance, if you struggle against positive flesh, you can disarm it by reminding yourself to rely upon Christ's life within you rather than your personal accomplishments (Philippians 3:7-8). Conversely, if you wrestle with negative flesh, you can disable it by renewing your mind with the truth that Christ loves and cares for you (Philippians 4:6-8). Remember that the flesh does not define who you are; it only shows what kinds of lies you are more apt to believe.

We should be aware of Satan's fleshly tactics to tempt us to sin. However, we should not discuss the flesh without reiterating the victory we have in Christ. You cannot improve or get rid of the flesh, and it can master you if you focus on it. Thus, God does not want you to dwell upon the flesh. Instead, He wants you to take comfort in the victory that He has already given you.

Christ—Our Source of Victory

Have you ever gone on a diet? What normally happens? Usually you discipline yourself to exercise and eat right. Over time, you achieve some success, but when you quit your diet, your body gains back some pounds. So you dedicate yourself to losing weight again, falling into a frustrating cycle. Worse, regardless of how hard you try to enhance your shape, your body remains in a constant state of decay, which means you cannot prevent the inevitable sags, wrinkles, and death.

Battling against fleshly urges of indwelling sin with your willpower is similar to dieting. You can try to defy temptation through self-effort, biblical principles, or accountability groups, but sin will never stop enticing you until you die. Your self-discipline may yield some temporary success, but eventually, stress, boredom, or fatigue will wear you down. The moment your self-effort gets weak, sin will pounce on you (1 Peter 5:8). God offers a better way to resist sin:

> For the grace of God has appeared, bringing salvation to all men, instructing us to deny ungodliness and worldly desires and to live sensibly, righteously, and godly in the present age (Titus 2:11-12).

Titus 2:11-12 says that the grace of God instructs you to live in a godly manner. It does not say that righteous behavior occurs through self-discipline, memorizing Scripture, or following principles. You cannot muster enough self-control to stop Satan. Instead, Paul writes that the goal of the Christian life is to "glory in Christ Jesus and put no confidence in the flesh" (Philippians 3:3). He also says, "For I know that nothing good dwells in me, that is, in my flesh; for the willing is present in me, but the doing of the good is not" (Romans 7:18). How do you give up your pride and allow God's grace to deliver you from temptation?

> I have been crucified with Christ; and it is no longer I who live, but Christ lives in me; and the life which I now

live in the flesh *I live by faith in the Son of God*, who loved
me and gave Himself up for me (Galatians 2:20).

This verse reveals one of the best blessings of being a Christian!
Instead of fighting sin with all your might, you can allow Christ
to do the fighting for you. He wants you to stop struggling, rest by
faith in His love, and let Him take over.

As an example, let's revisit Chuck's dilemma at the beginning
of this chapter. Remember how he got upset with his girlfriend,
Leah, for talking to Dan? If Chuck had allowed Christ to live
through him, he might have responded to his angry feelings by
thinking, *Why am I feeling this way? I am holy, so obviously these
angry and jealous thoughts are sin's attempt to control me. However,
Jesus freed me from sin's power. Lord, please take over and live Your
patience through me toward Leah right now.* If Chuck had continued to trust in Christ, he could have remained calm while Leah
talked to Dan.

Regardless of how you are tempted, sin can never offer anything superior to the unconditional love and acceptance that
you already have in Christ. Therefore, by comparison alone,
temptation is worthless. Sin can be very subtle, however, so Jesus
advises you to let go of your discipline and appropriate His
strength in dealing with fleshly enticements. He wants to help
you discern the lies that sin presents and remind you of His passionate love.

Jesus conquered sin forever when He died on the cross. Furthermore, His resurrection enabled Him to live His victory
through your life. Yet Christ cannot disarm temptation until you
stop trying to fight it by yourself.

Good Feelings Might Not Follow

Some Christians deny Christ's involvement with their sinful
struggles because they do not feel victorious over sin. The absence
of triumphant feelings, however, does not mean that Christ isn't

working in your life. Your emotions do not always follow the truth; they can be deceived rather easily.

For instance, when you watch a scary movie in the safety of a large theater, your feelings will respond to the fearful images in front of you. You react in terror while, in reality, you are completely safe. Your emotions respond to what you think about, and if you dwell upon anxious thoughts, feelings of fear and worry will develop. In addition, intense emotions can take time to subside before you feel at peace.

Satan knows that emotions can lie, so he will use them against you. Often, he will claim that you are not dead to sin because you can still feel his temptations. For this reason, spiritual truth will not become real to you until you learn to walk by faith. In *The Rest of the Gospel*, authors Greg Smith and Dan Stone explain why faith is so important against temptation:

> You are meant to be tempted, or there could be no such thing as faith. I'm not saying you are meant to fall to temptation.... God created beings that He has determined will operate by freedom, choice, and faith. And we are meant to have the consequences of our free choices.... God has not declared your soul or your body completely off-limits to Satan. There is only one place that is off-limits, where we are safe. That's our spirit union.... Jesus disarmed him [Satan] at the cross. He no longer has any power over you. The minute you see that he no longer has any power over you, isn't it amazing—you stop acting as if he has power over you.
>
> We're dead to sin, but the tempter isn't dead to us. He isn't meant to be dead to us, as long as this seen and temporal realm exists. You and I are meant to be in tension, the creative tension that temptation produces for faith responses.... We can spend our lives trying to hide and have very few faith experiences, or we can get out in the forefront and recognize that this is the way life works. In response to temptation, we learn to say, "I'm not meant to be controlled by my feelings and my thoughts.

I'm married to Jesus, and the only life that I want to have expressed through me is the life of my Husband."[3]

You may take a while to feel victorious against sinful desires because Satan does not quit tempting you. Your victory in Christ does not equal feeling free from temptation. Instead, Jesus set you free from having to yield to temptation. When you live by faith in Christ's strength, then sin eventually loses its appeal because you realize it has nothing beneficial to offer. In time, your feelings will follow as you renew your mind to the truth of His love.

Dealing with Sinful Deception in Dating

Now that you realize the reality of indwelling sin, let's uncover two ways that it tries to spoil your dating life. First, Satan has learned a secret method to tempt you into becoming so self-focused that you no longer desire to love another person. Second, he will use the flesh to simultaneously tempt you and your boyfriend or girlfriend, hoping to destroy your relationship through conflict.

Mind Games

Fleshly behavior is all about self: self-confidence, self-pity, self-condemnation, self-righteousness, self-indulgence, self-absorption, and so on. Whenever you act in these ways, you disregard God and the needs of others. Relationships fall apart if people concentrate on themselves. In contrast, humility cultivates intimacy between people.

> Do nothing from selfishness or empty conceit, but with humility of mind regard one another as more important than yourselves; do not merely look out for your own personal interests, but also for the interests of others (Philippians 2:3-4).

If humility, compassion, and honesty are rare characteristics in your relationships, you may have forgotten that an evil agent is at work against your mind. Arrogant or manipulative behavior does not happen by itself. Sin is actively at work to encourage you toward a self-centered attitude. In fact, sin is the cause of every pessimistic or selfish thought that enters your mind.

On the other hand, we know that God never gives you a negative thought because the Bible says that "He Himself does not tempt anyone" (James 1:13). In addition, "Therefore there is now no condemnation [disapproval] for those who are in Christ Jesus" (Romans 8:1). God always gives you positive and encouraging thoughts—even when He convicts you. Therefore, you can analyze your thoughts according to their characteristics and discern their origin.

Satan, however, does not give up easily. Instead, he disguises his temptations by speaking to your mind in the first person. *First person* is an English-language term. It describes sentences that use such pronouns as *I* or *me.* Satan knows that if you hear a thought with the words *I* or *me,* you will usually believe that you created the idea. Thus, he tricks you into thinking that you want to sin by tempting you with first-person thoughts.

Satan knows that his temptations would be easy to recognize if he said, *Hey you, wouldn't it be a great idea to have sex with your date tonight?* A temptation such as that is too obvious. Instead, he plants thoughts using first-person sentences, such as *I really want to have sex with my date tonight.* When you hear this idea, he hopes you believe that the thought is yours because of the words *I, me,* and *my.* Satan's trick is designed to make you think that you really want to act in an unholy way. In reality, Satan is pretending to be you.

Satan is no fool. He knows that he can most easily persuade you by staying undercover. Therefore, learn to examine your thoughts and determine who originates them. Whenever you think negative, immoral, selfish, proud, or anxious thoughts, Satan is the initiator.

Your union with Christ, however, gives Him the same ability to influence your thoughts. You can discern His voice, knowing that He always speaks to you with positive thoughts of peace, truth, and contentment. For instance, if a man dates a beautiful woman, Jesus might speak to his mind, *You don't need sex with her to be complete. You have everything you need in your spiritual marriage to Me.* Jesus could also speak in first-person thoughts, such as *I want to respect this woman, and I would rather wait for sex until marriage.*

Use this knowledge to remember that as a Christian, you are holy and righteous. Sin indwells your body, but that does not make you evil. Your true identity is someone who wants to do good (Romans 7:21).

His Flesh, Her Flesh

When a man and woman date one another, each of them can be tempted to sin. In addition, both harbor selfish flesh patterns, which can cause relational difficulties. Thus, in dating, if two people walk in the flesh, conflict and manipulative tactics can quickly destroy their relationship.

Ashley and I experienced the destructive effects of the flesh during our third month of dating. One Saturday, we had agreed to meet at my place at two o'clock, and I was looking forward to seeing her. Ashley called at lunch to say that she was on her way but had some errands to run first. Two o'clock came and went, however, and I sat staring at the clock, waiting for her to show up. With every minute, my anger intensified. She finally arrived after three o'clock, but by then, I was livid. I lit into her as she got out of her car. "Where have you been?"

"Running errands just as I told you," she shot back.

I expected Ashley to apologize. Instead, she casually walked passed me. I growled, "You said you would be here at two o'clock. Who do you think you are, showing up this late?"

Ashley replied, "I never said I'd be here by two o'clock. I said around two o'clock. Who are you to tell me what to do?" Within minutes, we were arguing as if we hated each other.

What caused such a heated quarrel? On the outside, it looks like a simple case of Ashley running late. Yet, if you could have read our minds, you would have heard all sorts of selfish thoughts, stirred up by Satan through the flesh:

The flesh urged Rob:	The flesh urged Ashley:
It's not fair for me to have to wait on Ashley.	I can do whatever I want.
Maybe Ashley doesn't care about me.	Why must I apologize? Rob's a jerk.
I won't date a girl who displeases me.	Rob should just get over it.

Notice how thoughts using *I* and *me* worked to instigate our conflict. What seemed like our desire to fight was actually dissension caused by Satan through the flesh. As Christians, Ashley and I did not truly want to argue. We deeply desired to let Christ love one another through us. However, we both chose to listen to the flesh and respond selfishly.

When a dating couple interacts, Satan uses the sinful flesh to destroy their relationship by tempting both individuals. That is how conflict starts. One person acts on a tempting thought and tries to control his or her date. And how do most people respond when someone tries to manipulate them? They also give in to temptation and start arguing, and soon they are trying to pummel one another's self-esteem. The one who dishes out the most rejection usually claims victory, but the relationship ends up in shambles.

How can you keep fleshly thoughts from corrupting your dating relationship? As we discussed earlier, you will not find the answer in your willpower or through adhering to relationship principles. Those methods offer only a temporary fix. Loving another person during conflict occurs as you allow Christ to live His love through you. When we yield to Jesus, He can reveal the selfish lies that Satan presents and replace them with His truth.

Let's see how the love of Christ could have overpowered the temptation for Ashley and me to argue.

> The flesh urged Rob: *It's not fair for me to have to wait.*
>
> Christ's love could prompt this response: *Sure, waiting on someone is no fun. But as a Christian, I no longer depend upon how a woman treats me—Jesus provides the acceptance that my heart needs. It would have been fine for me to ask Ashley why she was late and request her to show up on time. I had no excuse, however, to jump all over her in anger. The flesh deceived me with the temptation to protect my ego.*
>
> The flesh urged Ashley: *I can do whatever I want.*
>
> Christ's love could prompt this response: *I am free to make my own decisions, but Christ says that real love considers the needs of others. In a relationship, we are never free to do whatever we want. God calls us to seek the benefit of the other person. So rather than fall for the fleshly temptation to flaunt my independence, I will allow Christ to extend communication and cooperation through me.*

The flesh does not disappear when two Christians date each other. This means that whomever you date has indwelling sin influencing him or her. Should your boyfriend or girlfriend be ignorant of this fact, he or she may never realize why loving you is such a struggle. Someone who understands his or her union with Christ can let Jesus guard against Satan's destructive tricks.

The Good, the Bad, and the Fleshly

The goal of a dating relationship should be to discover what is real about another person. Sinful flesh resides within every human being and is one of the ugly realities that you must face. As you date someone, observe how he or she deals with temptation. Can your date recognize fleshly lies? Does he or she consistently depend upon Christ?

If your date does not recognize sin's influential ability, the flesh can easily deceive him or her. Moreover, your date may not know that Christ is his or her only source of victory against temptation. As a result, your date will fight sin in vain because his or her self-discipline won't last.

In addition, every person carries unique flesh patterns, such as passivity, pride, anxiety, the need to please people, or perfectionism. Other patterns include extreme behavior, such as rage, addictions, lust, or fear of commitment. Thus, once you are dating someone seriously, you may want to identify his or her struggles. Not only does this let you decide if you are willing to move forward but also effectively prepares you for the reality of living with that individual in a marriage.

When you can cherish someone, along with his or her irritating style of flesh, you learn to love a person just as he or she is. That is God's ultimate goal for a passionate dating relationship: that you love someone as Christ loves you—with the good, the bad, and the fleshly.

Personal Bible Study

1. Read Proverbs 16:2 and Romans 14:23. How does God determine whether your actions are sinful or holy?

2. Read 2 Corinthians 3:4-6 and 1 Corinthians 15:10. What is the secret of Paul's success? To whom should you credit any success in your life?

3. In Philippians 3:3-8, Paul says his achievements mean nothing compared to knowing Christ. In what ways might you rely upon your fleshly credentials more than on the love of Jesus?

4. How many times in Romans 7:15-25 do you find "sin" written as a noun? Sin is a separate entity, which attempts to negatively influence you. How can this truth change the way you view a temptation?

5. List the reasons for quarrels and strife given in James 4:1-3. In verses 4-8, how does James suggest we resist temptation?

6. Read Romans 7:24–8:2. Who is your only Source of victory over temptation? Why?

Group Discussion Questions

1. Discuss the benefit of understanding that sin is a separate entity from you.

2. Why can't you trust your emotions? How do you keep
   from making emotional dating decisions?

3. Name two ways that Satan uses the flesh to positively
   or negatively appeal to you.

4. Identify two pessimistic thoughts that Satan uses to discourage you about dating. Then, work together to find
   a Bible verse about God's love that refutes those negative thoughts.

5. Satan can whisper temptations using first-person statements designed to trick you. Discuss three examples.

6. Have a volunteer share a recent example of a dating
   conflict. As a group, discuss how the sinful flesh used
   selfish attitudes to tempt the couple to escalate their
   conflict. How could the love of Christ have diffused
   their selfish attitudes?

7

THE BOND
OF PASSION

:: :: ::

Discovering God's Design for Sex

*D*o you remember your first kiss? I sure do. I was 16 years old, standing by a river under a black sky filled with stars. Beside me was the most beautiful girl I had ever laid eyes on. We had successfully concealed ourselves from the counselors at our church youth camp. Hidden behind some trees, she looked at me, and I looked at her, then—BAM! Fireworks went off. The rush was overwhelming. My heart soared as our lips touched, and I felt that I had suddenly crossed over into manhood. Later, I told all of my buddies, and they jealously called me The Man. I had wooed my princess and won her kiss, but it felt so good that I couldn't get enough.

Consequently, our relationship turned into nothing but a smooch-fest. I would drive over to my girlfriend's house, go down to the basement, turn on the TV, and never look at it. Instead, we sat on the couch, trying to set a world record for the longest kiss. To a teenage boy, it was paradise. I couldn't imagine anything more fun in life. In my haze of pleasure, I believed that we would get married and our romance would last forever. The future seemed so glorious—until her mood changed one day. I showed up for another make-out session, but she answered the door and said, "All we ever do is kiss, and I'm tired of it. Our relationship is boring, and I don't want to see you anymore."

I was floored. My heart practically jumped out of my chest, and I begged her to reconsider. But she was adamant about breaking up, so I got back into my car and drove away, devastated. In that moment, I went from the King of Kissing to the Pauper of Pain. Without her affection, I felt as if a piece of me was missing. Nobody had warned me that a kiss, which felt so good, could hurt so much when taken away.

Have you ever experienced a similar situation? Did you give your heart to someone through a kiss, only to feel crushed when things didn't work out? Maybe you went all the way and gave your body sexually to another person. Did the bliss last when you stopped seeing each other? Like me, you probably discovered that considering the pain of withdrawal, sensual activity is not all you thought it would be.

Many singles fall into a dating pattern that involves physical affection followed by heartache. It happens when you date someone, go overboard sensually, spoil your relationship, and feel broken inside after you separate. I can relate to the emotional agony of this problem, and it distresses me to watch so many people blindly jump into the heat of sexual passion.

God made sex as a good gift, so why do people so often crave and misuse it? I believe that sex is appealing because each of us yearns for someone to accept us naked and unashamed. Our hearts long for a relationship where we can remove all of our defenses yet still have someone celebrate us for who we are. However, when we do not realize that Jesus Christ already loves us this passionately, we can view sex as the fulfillment to our hungry hearts. To make matters worse, our media bombards us with so much sensuality that we naturally get curious. Thus, sex can become the ultimate aspiration in a dating relationship.

God created sex, so nothing is wrong with it. We make it wrong by the way we choose to use it. Sex is for our good. However, if we don't understand how sex works, then mishandling it can cause us serious damage.

Sex Bonds People Together

The Bible clearly says to avoid sex outside of marriage (1 Thessalonians 4:3-8). Yet has anyone ever told you why? As a young single, I usually heard, "God says don't do it." This left a lot of confusion in my mind. If sex feels so good, then why should I have to wait for it? It's not fair for married couples to have all the fun.

Throughout high school and college, I attended several seminars that urged students to remain virgins. However, these campaigns focused on avoiding pregnancy or sexually transmitted diseases. The speakers never offered any real reasons to wait for sex. I didn't clearly understand the purpose of abstinence before marriage until years later when I was reading the apostle Paul's letter to the Corinthians.

The Christians in Corinth struggled to control their sexual desires because they lived in a culture that encouraged immorality. In their city, a certain pagan temple housed more than 1000 prostitutes, and people considered sex an act of worship. Similar to our modern society, the Corinthians made sexual pleasure a selfish act to engage in whenever they felt like it. Paul wrote the Corinthian Christians a letter to help them understand why God intended sex only for marriage.

> And don't you know that if a man *joins* himself to a prostitute, he becomes one body with her? For the Scriptures say, "The two are united into one." But the person who is *joined* to the Lord becomes one spirit with Him. Run away from sexual sin! No other sin so clearly affects the body as this one does. For sexual immorality is a sin against your own body (1 Corinthians 6:16-18 NLT).

In verse 16, Paul indicates that if a man has sex with a prostitute, he joins his body to hers. The key word in that verse is "joins." The original Greek word means "to cement or glue together firmly."[1] Paul is explaining that sex is a physical act that glues the bodies and souls of two people together. However, he wasn't referring only to sex with prostitutes. He meant that any couple who engages in sexual activity joins themselves together. More importantly, their bond is not a weak connection that breaks apart easily. Sex produces a bond that has the strength of superglue. It fastens a couple together so tightly that they cannot separate without causing damage to each other.

As a boy, I discovered the power of a superglue bond when I built model airplanes. Occasionally, I ran out of the toy airplane adhesive and tried to use superglue as a substitute. One day, I got careless and accidentally bonded two of my fingers together. I was shocked when I couldn't get them apart. I pulled and pried, but they were fused. I finally had to tear them apart by painfully ripping my skin. My fingers were left raw and wounded. This is similar to what happens when two people have sex and then break up. They fuse their hearts and souls together, and then suffer agonizing damage when they separate.

Maybe you doubt that sex actually bonds people together. If so, talk to any man or woman who has broken up after having intercourse. They will verify that their emotional and physical bond was real because immense pain occurred when they tried to separate. What they thought was harmless kissing and touching had literally cemented their hearts together. For this reason, you must take physical activity seriously in a dating relationship. Much more is happening than you can see or feel. By being careless, you can intertwine yourself with someone without even realizing it.

If sex didn't bond people together, you could make love and never think twice about it. Yet God designed sex to join people, and you will experience consequences if you have sex and then try to walk away. This doesn't apply only to intercourse either. You can also damage yourself through less intense involvement.

I remained a virgin until I married, but I still suffered pain from my physical activity in dating. My three most agonizing breakups occurred after I had been very sensual with my girlfriends. My heart felt devastated after each separation. In contrast, I broke up with another girl with whom I had had no sexual involvement, and the emotional pain was negligible. Therefore, understand the risk you take if you get physically active with your boyfriend or girlfriend. *You are not playing with fire; you are playing with superglue.*

What Is Sex?

The definition of sex broadens when you realize that all sexual activity joins two people together. You cannot limit sex to just intercourse because any type of physical touching starts the bonding process. For instance, a man does not hold a woman's hand to say, "I hate you." He holds her hand to quietly say, "I like you, and I want to explore a relationship with you." Then, if he kisses her, they will emotionally bond a little more. Should they get involved with kissing erotically, touching one another's sensual areas, or having oral sex, their hearts and souls will begin to firmly unite.

The further a couple goes physically, the tighter they bond emotionally, and the more damage their hearts and minds will suffer if they separate. That's why developing a sexual relationship without the lifetime commitment of marriage is unwise. You jeopardize bonding your heart to someone who may not stay with you. Even if you are engaged, the possibility for separation still exists.

This does not mean that all physical affection in dating is bad. A romantic touch can be beneficial when it reinforces the spiritual, emotional, and intellectual connection that a couple has *already* developed. For example, if a guy tells his girlfriend, "I really like you," but he refuses to hug her, she would probably consider him a hypocrite. By touching her, he confirms his interest in their relationship. Therefore, it is okay for a couple to express themselves physically but not at the expense of bonding and breaking their hearts.

Jesus wants physical activity to profit your relationship rather than destroy it. So be aware of what sex can do to your heart. In the next chapter, we will discover how Christ can help you decide what level of physical involvement is appropriate.

The Consequences of Breaking a Sexual Bond

In her early twenties, Serena slept with several different men. She couldn't resist the boost to her self-esteem when a man desired her sexually. She was young and free, and a committed relationship was the last thing on her mind. When she became bored with one guy, she simply broke up with him and flirted with another. When she accidentally got pregnant, Serena chose an abortion to solve the problem. She didn't realize that her sexual carelessness was deadening her heart's ability to experience real intimacy and commitment.

Later, at age 28, Serena began to ponder her future. Staying single forever no longer excited her, so she decided to look for a husband and settle down. She started visiting a local church and hit it off with a guy named Doug. While they dated, Serena curbed her sexual activity with Doug and kept her sensual past a secret. She figured her new behavior exhibited maturity and felt ready for marriage when Doug proposed after nine months of dating.

Serena joyously anticipated a wonderful life with Doug, but her hopes vanished on their honeymoon. Whenever Serena tried to make love to her new husband, memories of her abortion and previous sexual partners flooded her mind. Guilt and shame tortured her thoughts and hindered her from focusing on Doug. Serena's inability to enjoy sexual intimacy deeply disappointed her. She kept the frustration to herself, but a familiar desire began to arise from it.

Serena had always avoided relational pain by running from it, so the urge to abandon her marriage and start over began to entice her. She tried to fight the feeling because she cared for Doug.

However, when he asked her for sex, she wanted to run away. Serena hoped the problem would disappear over time, but instead, her frustration increased. Five months into her marriage, Serena deserted Doug and began a new, desperate search for fulfillment.

In our culture, Satan has successfully redefined sex as a pleasure drug or a seductive method to control a relationship. Sex, however, was never designed for these purposes. God made it to bond people together in marriage, and people forfeit their ability to enjoy it when they abuse His gift.

As we saw in Serena's case, if you get involved in premarital sex, you can deteriorate your heart's future capacity to experience intimacy. This problem is comparable to breaking your leg. Your body will heal, but your joints and tendons do not grow back as strong as before. As a result, you can never again enjoy certain activities to the degree that you did previously. Likewise, your heart is emotionally fragile and can be easily damaged. Therefore, if you repeatedly bond yourself to others sexually and then break those bonds, you cannot expect your heart to be capable of complete intimacy in the future. It will heal, but it will never be the same.

Some singles disagree and ask me, "What about those people who say they can have sex without feeling anything for the other person? Can they avoid consequences?" The answer is no. People who abuse sex always suffer injury to themselves. God says that anyone who engages in sex outside of marriage destroys his or her own body (1 Corinthians 6:18; Ephesians 4:17-19). No one can indulge in carnal sensuality without experiencing at least one of the following repercussions:

- Your heart disconnects from people, and you lose the ability to feel.
- You deaden your ability to stay committed in a future relationship.
- You run the high risk of sexually transmitted disease, pregnancy, or physical abuse.

- Your heart is numbed toward real intimacy when you truly want it in the future.
- Your immorality destroys other people's ability to trust or respect you.
- You carry a burden of guilt and shame from taking advantage of another person.
- Your sex life eventually becomes boring and routine.

All of these consequences carry a high price because you cannot enjoy sex with a damaged heart or a damaged body. The ugly problems that sexually transmitted diseases cause are easy to understand. However, finding sexual intimacy is even more frustrating when your heart is dead or distracted. The superglue power of intercourse rips away a piece of your heart when you break a sexual bond, and your heart may never completely recover.

God does not forbid singles to touch each other, but when you begin sexual contact you initiate His bonding process. To avoid damaging yourself, keep physical activity in line with the commitment level of your relationship. By doing so, you prevent bonding your heart to someone who may decide to leave. Also, you allow your relationship a better chance of developing communication, patience, and sacrificial love—elements necessary for a lifelong marriage.

Sex may bond two people together, but it does not guarantee them a good relationship. Instead, their character, relational maturity, and dependence upon Jesus Christ determine the quality of their relationship.

Why Sexual Attraction Is Good

God did not invent sex just to give people a pleasant, tingling sensation. His primary intention was to illustrate the intimate, joyful union that exists spiritually between Jesus Christ and you (1 Corinthians 6:17). *God created you with the capacity for sexual passion so that you could comprehend Christ's passion for you.* Your physical attraction to someone on earth represents Jesus' excitement toward you. Sexual passion is a picture of His desire. Look at how He describes you as His bride:

> Then the King will desire your beauty.... The King's daughter is all glorious within; Her clothing is interwoven with gold. She will be led to the King in embroidered work (Psalm 45:11-14).

> You have ravished my heart, my treasure, my bride. I am overcome by one glance of your eyes, by a single bead of your necklace. How sweet is your love, my treasure, my bride! How much better it is than wine! Your perfume is more fragrant than the richest of spices. Your lips, my bride, are as sweet as honey. Yes, honey and cream are under your tongue (Song of Solomon 4:9-11 NLT).

These verses show that Jesus loves you more than just as a friend. You captivate Him. Furthermore, you experience a taste of His intimate love if you share sexual delight with someone in a marriage relationship. The joy that a husband and wife express for each other portrays the delight and satisfaction that Christ feels about you. Jesus will even work through the physical touch of another person to get His point across to you. For example, I have a good friend, Joe, who once told me that sometimes when his wife, Angela, hugs him, he can sense Christ say, *Joe, you may feel Angela hugging you right now, but actually it is Me hugging you through her. I am so glad that you belong to Me, and I love you.*

Don't let this idea sound weird to you. Christ's passion for you is not some strange sexual-spiritual kind of love. Rather, Jesus feels an intense devotion and joy in His relationship with you. He thinks you're cool. He thinks you're beautiful. He thinks you're special. This idea may be hard to grasp, but Jesus is more delighted with you than an earthly husband is with his wife. That's why God created sex for marriage—to give you insight into the amazing pleasure that Christ feels in His union with you. Therefore, sex should always be respected as a divine gift.

God has a second purpose for sex: to produce total intimacy in marriage. Two spouses cannot experience oneness unless they share in sexual intercourse. Sex invites a husband and wife to accept each other naked, unashamed, and uninhibited. It offers an environment in which they are free to be themselves and joyfully bond in the most meaningful way possible. Our hearts crave this kind of intimacy, and sex in marriage is one of God's instruments to meet that need.

Dating serves as the spark to motivate two people to pursue the path toward marriage. As a single man and woman captivate each other, they want to begin a relationship. Their sex drives propel them to discover more about one another. Then, when they encounter the initial difficulties of communication and friendship, their sexual interest can encourage them to keep working through the problems. Thus, sexual attraction is an important aspect of dating relationships. Without it, singling out one person for intimacy would be boring and lifeless.

For most couples, a physical desire occurs when they initially meet. For a few, the attraction evolves over time. Regardless of when it happens, a mutual sexual attraction needs to develop eventually, or a dating couple will not enjoy intimacy in a marriage. Romance is an essential part of oneness, and a marriage devoid of physical closeness is a miserable experience.

Therefore, guys, don't believe the lie that Christian men are supposed to marry pious, unattractive women. That doesn't fit within the context of how Jesus loves you as His bride. You exhilarate Christ, so He wants you to be thrilled about the woman you choose to marry. He wants her unique beauty to satisfy you completely (Proverbs 5:18-19). Thus, if you have not met a Christian woman who possesses integrity and sexually attracts you, keep looking. Do not settle for anyone just to get married.

Likewise, ladies, treasure your beauty, femininity, and purity. To Jesus, you were worth His sacrifice, and He wants you to find a husband who will treat you in the same way. A man is not worth marrying if he will not cherish you and give himself up for you.

So avoid the losers who simply want to use your body for sex. Wait to marry a man who is so wild about you that he is willing to restrain his desires and offer you a lifetime commitment.

What Satan Doesn't Want You to Know About Sex

Satan always takes God's good gifts and twists them into something destructive. He does this with food, nature, and especially sex. Let's look at some truths about sex that he does not want you to know.

God Created Sex as a Celebration

Satan tries to confuse many singles by advertising that forbidden or kinky sex is the most satisfying kind. You see this evil message propagated by movies, books, and TV. Believe me, it's a lie. Hot sex does not happen by using special techniques or having secret affairs. Fantastic sex occurs when a man and a woman share uninhibited romance in a committed marriage.

God made sex as a delightful celebration between a husband and a wife. It is one of the most personal and intimate ways to say, "Thank you for loving me." Thus, when a couple marries, God wants them to relish their sex life and enjoy it often (Ecclesiastes 9:9; 1 Corinthians 7:3-5; Ephesians 5:28-29). He invites them to be as sensual and free as they desire.

This should not dishearten you or make you jealous about refraining from sex as a single. Rather, I want to encourage you to pursue sex for the right reasons. God knew what He was doing when He created it. Do not think that sex between Christian spouses is supposed to be boring and prudish. God designed sex in marriage to be a blast, and when you share unreserved passion in a committed marriage, it will blow your mind.

Sex Is Just a Piece of the Pie

Sex is an integral part of marriage. However, you need also to be aware that if you get married, sex will become a small piece of the total relationship. Married couples do not have sex around the clock. Most wives desire sex much less frequently than their husbands do. Therefore, guys, you will have to learn to control your urges within marriage as well as without.

In addition, sex is not a constant party that keeps spouses together. It is a brief rendezvous that celebrates their love. Neither can sex make a marriage better. Instead, it serves as a gauge for the quality of a couple's communication, sacrifice, cooperation, and friendship. If you are not cherishing one another in respect and submission, your sex life will deteriorate.

Furthermore, frequent sex only adds up to a few hours during the week. When you are married, you live with someone 24 hours a day. Thus, the nonsexual parts of your relationship, such as cooperation with chores, raising children, and trusting Christ together, play larger roles in the success of your marriage.

Newlyweds Are Not Sexually Compatible

Some singles assume that all of their sexual fantasies will instantly come true on their wedding night. This lie from Satan leads to disappointment because no married couple has immediate sexual compatibility. Great sex does not happen by itself. Husbands and wives must discuss, develop, and practice it. Some couples adjust more quickly than others, but most couples need many months before they are comfortable in bed together. This is completely normal.

Thus, do not expect fantastic sex on your honeymoon. You will need to research the subject, go very slowly, practice often, and talk things out until you understand what brings pleasure to each other. You can study books about how to improve your sexual technique, but the real key is learning to mutually sacrifice. Your sex life will stink if you try to force your spouse to do what you want. The real delight occurs when the pleasure of the other person becomes your main focus.

You Cannot Give Sex a Test Drive

It is surprising how many Christian singles choose to move in with their boyfriends or girlfriends. Satan motivates people to "test drive" their relationship by reasoning, "If we live together, we can see how well we get along. Then, if we don't like each other, we can easily break up without the entanglements of marriage." This may sound like wise advice, but I must bluntly state that living together makes no sense whatsoever.

The truth is that if you live in the same house, sleep in the same bed, pay the same bills, and have sex with your boyfriend or girlfriend, you are already married. The difference is that you are too selfish to make your marriage official with a commitment. Remember that sex bonds people together; a paper marriage license doesn't. If you move in together and start fooling around, you will bond your hearts together just as a married couple does. Once you bond sexually, there is no turning back. You may think that moving in together is a relationship test, but in reality, you have already joined yourself to someone. Should you decide to break up, you will suffer the same emotional consequences as any divorcing couple does.

On the other hand, some singles, usually women, believe that living together will increase their chances of getting their boyfriends to marry them. They rationalize that a little sex will convince him to get serious. However, moving in together does not encourage anyone to commit. Instead, it discourages people from getting married because they can have all of the sex, financial support, and companionship they want for free. In their minds, why should they marry when they already have everything they want with no strings attached?

Moving in together indicates that a couple wants all of the positives of marriage (including sex, intimacy, security, and companionship) without having to invest in it. Yet people cannot obtain the benefits of marriage unless they selflessly commit themselves to another person. You cannot have real intimacy without sacrificial love and a commitment. These qualities are absent when a couple lives together.

Cohabitation encourages a relationship to fail because it is founded on selfishness. In essence, pleasure and convenience are more important than the other person's well-being. Thus, you cannot live with someone and justifiably say, "I love you." If you really love that person, then you will either get married or date without having sex.

Sex Can Destroy You

Lastly, Satan wants you to think that sex is just harmless fun, but he knows it is an act of bonding. Therefore, he will attempt to use sexual passion to put you in *bondage*. This could include bondage to a bad relationship, pornography, homosexuality, or romantic fantasies. Sexual experiences may feel good, but the pleasure can easily become addicting. Satan's deception about sex is widespread, so the next chapter will deal with sensual temptation and how Christ can guide you to make wise decisions about physical activity in your relationship.

Thank God for Sex

Regardless of Satan's attempt to distort our understanding of sex, we are blessed to have such a wonderful gift from God. The Lord intends sex for our good, and nothing else can bond two people so intimately. Therefore, cherish your ability to express physical desire for another person, knowing that sex represents Christ's passionate desire for you. Look forward to celebrating the power of passionate sex when you are married—it will be worth the wait.

Personal Bible Study

1. Romans 1:21-29 and 13:13-14 give a snapshot of how sex was misused earlier in history. What do these verses say caused the immoral behavior? In what ways does our current culture similarly abuse God's bonding process of sex?

2. What attitude about sex does 1 Corinthians 7:3-5 suggest for a husband and wife? Why is it important for a married couple to enjoy sex regularly?

3. Proverbs 5:18-19 encourages three attitudes about sex in marriage. What are they? Are you surprised to see in the Bible that God openly advocates sex?

4. Read Song of Solomon 4. How do you feel when you read about a husband so enraptured sexually with his wife? What do you think this reflects about the intimacy of their relationship?

5. In 1 Thessalonians 4:3-8, what is God's will concerning sex?

6. Read Hebrews 13:4. Now that you have read chapter 7, why do you think God designed sex for a marriage relationship only?

Group Discussion Questions

1. God created sex as a superglue bonding process. How does this knowledge change your view of sexual activity in dating?

2. Chapter 7 lists seven potential repercussions of having sex outside of marriage. Have you seen anyone suffer these consequences? Identify other consequences of sexual immorality not listed in this chapter.

3. Allow each group member to define what kissing in a dating relationship means to him or her. Then discuss how kissing changes the atmosphere of a relationship.

4. Talk about the parallels between sexual passion in marriage and the passionate love that Jesus has for every person.

5. Consider the reasons why God would want a Christian single to marry someone who attracts him or her sexually.

6. Discuss why living together damages a relationship. What are some common lies that deceive couples into choosing cohabitation?

8

CONFRONTING
COUNTERFEIT PASSION

:: :: ::

Dealing with Sexual Temptation

$\mathcal{A}$s Dennis parked his car in front of Sonya's apartment, their conversation fell silent. It was the end of their third date, and their new relationship appeared to be going well. Their talk at dinner had been stimulating, and a mutual attraction seemed evident as they gazed into each other's eyes over dessert. Now they found themselves stuck in that awkward parting moment at the end of a date.

Dennis's heart pounded. He wondered how to say goodnight. Should he kiss Sonya? She was beautiful, and he felt tempted to see how far he could go with her. Yet their relationship was just beginning, and Dennis wanted to respect Sonya. Would he come across as forward or disrespectful if he initiated physical activity? His clammy hands gripped the steering wheel as he pondered his dilemma.

Meanwhile, Sonya sat nervously, staring out the window. Would Dennis try to kiss her? She really liked him, but it was only their third date. If they kissed now, would Dennis expect something more on their next date? Would he lose interest in her if she discouraged any physical activity? She hated these uneasy moments....

When you feel physically attracted to your date, what should you do? Is it okay to kiss or caress? How far is too far? Should you avoid sex even if you truly love each other? Furthermore, how can anyone remain a virgin in our sex-crazed society? Christian singles struggle with these questions every day. If everyone around you is sexually active, how do you resist temptation and exhibit self-control in dating? Is there still hope if you have fallen sexually in a past relationship? This chapter will help you deal with these issues.

Foremost, let's remember from the previous chapter that God is not against sex. Instead, He created sex to joyfully bond two people together in marriage. Sex outside of marriage, however, will cause harmful consequences to you (1 Corinthians 6:18). So how do you resist immoral temptations in your dating life? First, you need to understand how sexual temptation originates, since resisting sex in the wrong way can actually weaken your restraint. Second, Jesus wants you to realize that victory over sensuality occurs as you allow Him to fight the battle for you.

The Origin of Sexual Temptation

God created your body with the capacity for sexual pleasure, but He does not place desires within you for immoral sexual behavior. As we saw in chapter 6, Satan uses indwelling sin to entice you into evil behavior. He tempts you through the flesh to pursue sexual fantasies or illicit affairs. Satan will even say that you need sensuality for biological reasons. That is a lie because you are not an animal who engages in sex out of instinct. You are a human being who has complete control over your sexual appetite. Therefore, when you are tempted with lustful thoughts, recognize that those desires are not yours.

Satan knows that feelings of loneliness, boredom, depression, or rejection can make you vulnerable to sensual desires. When you feel down, he will urge you to seek relief through sexual behavior, pornography, soap operas, or romance novels. To show how Satan subtly attempts to entice your mind, review the following abbreviated list of sexual thought patterns. When you feel bored, disappointed, or frustrated, do you sense the following urges?

- If I could just have sex, then I would be happy.
- I need a quick escape, so I'll look at pornography.
- Guys ignore me, so maybe I need to flirt more often or dress seductively.
- Dating is hard; maybe I should try an alternate lifestyle.
- Maybe I should lose myself in a steamy romance novel.

All of these tempting thoughts are Satan's efforts to control you through sex. Notice how he camouflages himself by using first-person sentences containing *I, my,* and *me.* Satan wants to make you think that you are the one who wants sex. Under this disguise, he receives much less resistance from you when he poses a temptation. Then, once you experience the pleasurable feelings, you might become hooked. Satan hopes to lead you into addiction to sexual passion so that you disregard the pure passion of Christ.

Self-Effort Does Not Work

We were born with hearts that require constant, unconditional love, and Jesus is the only Person who accepts us regardless of our behavior. However, if we do not allow Christ to satisfy our longing, Satan will quickly promote destructive substitutes, especially sexual excitement. He wants to make us dependent upon anything other than Jesus.

Furthermore, our hunger for love can overpower our self-discipline, common sense, or motivation to follow a godly principle. Our need for love is stronger than our dedication to wisdom or rules. For this reason, many Christian singles succumb to poor dating decisions. They crave acceptance so much that they are willing to pursue any dating relationship that offers some approval, even if it involves premarital sex, manipulation, or lust.

Their love-starved hearts settle for whatever comfort they can find most quickly.

Unfortunately, many Christians try to resist immoral temptation by memorizing biblical principles, using their willpower, or joining accountability groups. These methods may sound godly and helpful, but they are ineffective against carnal desires. Let's examine why these three techniques do not work and then discuss our true Source of freedom from temptation.

Practicing Principles Makes You Prone to Sin

Have you ever heard about a pastor caught in a sexual scandal or a music minister who confessed to an affair with a choir member? These problems happen in the modern church, but these religious men and women generally know biblical principles better than anyone else does. They could quote numerous Scriptures and guidelines that advise abstaining from sex outside of marriage. But these leaders still give in to immorality. Why don't they follow the biblical principles they preach?

The apostle Paul explained why rules encourage sin: "I would not have come to know sin except through the Law; for I would not have known about coveting if the Law had not said, 'You shall not covet.' But sin, taking opportunity through the commandment, produced in me coveting of every kind; for apart from the Law sin is dead" (Romans 7:7-8).

Paul states that rules actually increase sin's power to tempt you because if laws didn't exist, you wouldn't know what sin was. Furthermore, the law includes much more than the laws God gave to Israel through Moses and the prophets. It includes any regulation that you try to obey through your self-effort, such as a principle, a guideline, or even a standard that you create for yourself. If you put yourself under a law against a temptation, you invite sin to tempt you in that area (1 Corinthians 15:56).

Think about the highway speed limit laws, for example. When you drive, you see signs posted that govern how fast you should travel. To follow the law, you must obey these rules. Let's be honest, though. What happens when you see a speed limit sign? If it says 55, don't you usually feel tempted to drive 60 or 65 and hope you don't get caught? What brought the temptation of speeding to your mind? The rule on the sign. If there were no signs, you would not know what speeding is. Since the rules exist, Satan gets the opportunity to whisper, *That law is ridiculous and confines the way I want to drive.* As you pass by more signs, he argues, *Forget these rules. I can do whatever I want.* Eventually, you agree that the driving rule is restrictive, so you punch the gas pedal and fly down the road. Then, if you feel convicted, you try to rationalize your speeding with an excuse, such as *I was running late.*

Does this suggest that rules and principles are worthless? No, rules can benefit society by preventing chaos and guiding people away from harm. However, when you became a Christian, God freed you from living by the law (Romans 6:14; Galatians 3:24-25). Your acceptance to Him is no longer determined by following rules. You are now accepted and controlled through the unconditional love of Christ (2 Corinthians 5:14). You can live by trying to obey rules, but you will only give Satan more opportunity to wear you down with temptation.

Human Willpower Will Wear You Out

Jesus was not joking when He said, "The spirit is willing, but the flesh is weak" (Mark 14:38). Nevertheless, you may beg to differ. You might feel very confident in your self-discipline. When the Bible says, "Abstain from sexual immorality" (1 Thessalonians 4:3), you may feel sure that you can keep yourself pure.

You may believe that you can fight temptation through self-discipline, but why has no human ever had the discipline to keep the Ten Commandments? It is just a short list of rules (Exodus 20:1-17). If you have enough willpower, you should be able to obey them, right? According to God, however, not one human has ever been able to consistently follow His laws (Romans 3:23; James 2:10). Every person except Jesus has failed miserably.

When it comes to human self-restraint, we must admit our weakness because sin has corrupted our willpower. Furthermore, sin has rendered our self-discipline so ineffective that we eventually yield to whatever temptation we focus on. For instance, if a man tells himself, *I will not lust after the pretty secretary at my office,* that woman will become the focus of his mind. Satan will tempt him with lustful thoughts whenever she passes by his desk. Initially, the man may resist. Over time, however, he will exert a lot of mental energy, trying not to think about the secretary. Eventually, he will tire of keeping up his guard. Worn out, he will gaze at his secretary and give in to lustful temptation. His willpower may last longer than other men, but he will never find the strength to hold out forever.

If you focus on avoiding sexual temptation, your concentration will wear you out that much more quickly. That's why people who try to live by self-denial or strict behavior usually wind up frustrated and defeated. The apostle Paul said, "These rules may seem wise because they require strong devotion, humility, and severe bodily discipline. But they have no effect when it comes to conquering a person's evil thoughts and desires" (Colossians 2:23 NLT).

The Inability of Accountability

Many singles wisely acknowledge their weak willpower but then fight temptation by asking another person to help them. Sometimes this other person is called an "accountability partner." Generally, you meet with this person weekly or monthly to discuss your struggles and to strategize how you can more righteously behave.

The problem with human accountability, however, is that another Christian cannot make you do the right thing. Just like you, every Christian is imperfect and struggles with temptation. He or she might be older or have known the Lord longer, but seniority does not correlate with spiritual maturity or superior self-control. Older men and women sin just as often as younger people do. Therefore, another believer can encourage you, but he or she cannot improve your willpower because you are still responsible to make your own choices.

God does not want you to depend upon other imperfect humans to help you fight your temptations. Are accountability partners useless? No. Sharing your struggles with a caring friend can benefit both of you. Don't expect, however, that account-ability to rules or another imperfect person will give you victory over temptation. Jesus says that He wants to protect and strengthen you (2 Corinthians 12:9-10; Ephesians 3:16). Let's discuss the victory that He has already won for us.

Christ—the Answer Against Temptation

When Jesus walked the earth, the religious leaders constantly persecuted Him for breaking their rules. For example, Jesus healed a crippled man on the Sabbath. Despite this miracle, the religious leaders gave Him little appreciation. Instead, they accused Jesus of disobeying the Scripture, citing that He worked on their holy day of rest (John 9:15-17).

Jesus responded to them, "You search the Scriptures because you believe they give you eternal life. But the Scriptures point to Me! Yet you refuse to come to Me so that I can give you this eternal life" (John 5:39-40 NLT). Jesus meant that God did not intend for the Bible to be a list of rules about how to behave righteously. The Bible points us to Christ so that He can live His holiness through us. By itself, a principle or rule cannot cause good behavior. Truly loving behavior occurs when we trust Jesus to live His love through us. For this reason, Jesus said, "Abide in Me…for apart from Me you can do nothing" (John 15:4-5).

Instead of fighting temptation with your willpower, let Jesus handle the problem for you. This may sound like an artificial solution, but it is not. Let's quickly review part of chapter 6 to understand how He can live the victory through you:

   1. When you became a Christian, God crucified and removed your old sin nature. You are now dead to sin's

control. You can still be tempted, but sin can no longer command you (Romans 6:6).

2. God filled you with the righteous nature of Jesus Christ. Your spirit has been perfected, and you are a new creation, holy in God's sight (2 Corinthians 5:17,21).

3. Jesus dwells in your spirit; therefore, He can live His perfect life through you by making His desires your desires (Galatians 2:20; Psalm 37:4).

4. Because Christ lives in you, He can resist worldly urges for you whenever you allow Him (Titus 2:11-14).

As a Christian, you are no longer a sinner struggling to be good. You are now a righteous person who still has the choice to sin. For this transformation to become a reality in your life, however, you must act on it by faith. Faith is walking in agreement with whatever God says is true. If God says that you are dead to sin, then you have the choice to agree with Him. If God says that Jesus can live His life through you, then your faith allows Him to do so.

When you are tempted sexually, Jesus understands the difficult battle you face. He lived on earth for 33 years and ministered as a single adult among prostitutes and corrupt men. In addition, Satan tempted Christ, but Christ never sinned. Jesus always saw through Satan's deceit. In the same way, Jesus wants to expose Satan's schemes and resist your temptations for you. Your spiritual Husband knows that your willpower is ineffective. Therefore, He wants to be your Source of resistance. No temptation exists that Jesus cannot handle for you. He knows the difficulty of your struggles and asks you to give the battle to Him. How do you give up the battle and let Jesus work through you?

Think back to the speeding illustration earlier in this chapter. Remember that when you drive a car under your willpower, you eventually drive too fast and break the law. However, most cars have an option called cruise control, which removes the need for your willpower. By relying on the cruise control function of your vehicle, you allow it to effortlessly maintain the proper speed for you. All you have to do is turn it on, relax, and let it do the work. Letting Christ live through you is similar to driving with cruise control. He becomes your willpower and maintains the proper behavior for you by strengthening you "with His glorious power so that you will have all the patience and endurance you need" (Colossians 1:11 NLT). By faith, you ask Jesus to live His life through you. You remind yourself that God has removed sin's authority over you and that Jesus loves you passionately. He is your Life, and you trust Him for strength, wisdom, and self-control in every situation.

I'm not saying that God is your copilot. When you ask Christ to live His life through yours, you give up on yourself completely and let Him take full control. By yielding in faith, you exchange your weak willpower for His perfect self-control, patience, and kindness.

Christ living through you may be a hard idea to grasp, so let me give you a real-life example. Occasionally, I felt discouraged as I struggled to finish writing this book. The process was very frustrating, and sometimes Satan tempted me to pursue cheap relief while I sat alone at my computer. He whispered to my mind using first-person thoughts. *If I punch a few buttons on my keyboard, Internet porn could help me escape my frustration in seconds.* Instantly, I felt a powerful desire well up within my body to follow this temptation. So how did I escape this dilemma?

First, I did not hang large signs in my office that read, "Principle #1—Do not look at Internet porn!" Keeping a rule in my face against pornography would have only weakened my resolve by constantly reminding me about it. Second, I did not call another Christian and ask him to help me resist the temptation. Instead, I remembered that Jesus wanted to handle the problem for me. I could sense Him say, *Rob, My unconditional love for you is much better than any pictures of sleazy women who don't care about you. You can choose to look at that trash, but it will only hurt you.*

Pornography is a hideous lie from Satan, designed to put you in bondage to sex. I know that you can't resist it, so allow Me to live My self-control through you. You are dead to sin's control. I am now your Life, and I don't have any difficulty resisting porn. Enjoy My love, and let Me handle this temptation (see Romans 6:8-14; 2 Corinthians 4:11; Galatians 2:20).

Meanwhile, I could feel my body urging me to give in, but I mentally responded in faith, *Jesus, You are right. You never sinned, so pornography is no problem for You to resist. By Your death and resurrection, I am dead to my sinful flesh that wants to look at porn. Since You are my life, You take over and live Your wisdom through me. A naked woman on a computer screen doesn't love me. Pornography doesn't compare to Your unconditional love.* As I acknowledged this truth, my frustration eased, and the desire to look at Internet trash vanished—the temptation soon disappeared.

Let me emphasize that saying no to temptation will never set you free because it makes you focus on sin even more. You can only resist temptation when you hand over the problem to Christ. No temptation is too strong for His perfect love and wisdom. As you let Him live through you, you will experience victory over sexual temptation.

The Danger of Pornography and Romantic Fantasies

Since pornography and romantic fantasies pose such a big threat to the welfare of your dating life, let's briefly pause to understand the danger of these widespread temptations. We learned in the previous chapter that God created sex to firmly bond two people together. However, two people do not have to be together for the bonding process to take place. Your heart can be tricked into bonding with someone through sexual or romantic fantasies.

Men who fill their minds with sexual images or thoughts commonly fall into this trap. Pornography can become a drug that a man uses to find quick relief from his daily frustrations. The temptation to lust after erotic pictures of models seems easier than building a real relationship with a woman.

However, when a man looks at pornography, he can form a sexual bond to a woman who is not physically with him. As he gazes at her image, he unwittingly tricks his heart to seek fulfillment from a woman who does not love him. Initially, the ability to control pleasure through his fantasy may convince the man that pornography is satisfying. Through this process, though, that man may not realize how the pornographic fantasy silently destroys his self-esteem.

Consider the truth. Strippers and nude centerfold models do not love the men who look at them. Instead, those immoral women selfishly use men to make money or boost their egos. When a man looks at pornography, the women in the photos seem to entice, *I want you.* In reality, however, the man can't have her.

Consequently, a man can feel empty and ashamed after he fantasizes about a woman. He concludes, *I want her, but she is not here with me. Why can't I have a woman like her? I must not be worthy of love.* Pornography degrades a man's self-worth because fantasy relationships promote a sense of guilt, secret shame, and feelings of inadequacy.

Pornography also produces unrealistic expectations about sex in relationships. As a man lusts after pictures of naked women, he wrongly assumes that the best kind of woman is perfectly proportioned and offers constant pleasure. Lust classifies a woman as a sex *object* who should fulfill a man's selfish desires instead of a precious *person* to be loved sacrificially.

Sexual addiction can entrap a man if flesh patterns of fantasy and masturbation become deeply rooted in his mind and emotions. In these cases, Christian counseling may be required to help break the bondage. A counselor can uncover the lustful lies that a man believes and help him source his acceptance and significance from Christ rather than from a sexy woman (for more information about counseling, see chapter 10).

Many women also struggle with addictions to porn. In addition, they can fall prey to addictive consequences when they read romance novels, watch soap operas and romantic movies, or fantasize about men. These actions constitute emotional pornography. When a woman feels lonely or insecure, Satan may tempt her to dream of a man to rescue her from problems and fulfill her heart. Amorous affairs in cheap romance novels or romantic movies provide the fantasies to escape her troubles. The pleasure from these daydreams, however, is temporary and promotes an unrealistic ideal of relationships. An imperfect man cannot fulfill a woman's need for unconditional acceptance. More importantly, romantic fantasies fail to satisfy a woman's deep longing for love. She can daydream all day long, but her fantasies won't improve her reality. For that reason, her heart can fall further into emptiness, discontent, or depression. Meanwhile, Jesus is trying to tell her that He has already rescued her with His love.

You cannot spend time lusting in your mind and walk away unscathed. The apostle Paul says, "Flee immorality. Every other sin that a man commits is outside the body, but the immoral man sins against his own body" (1 Corinthians 6:18). Falling prey to sexual fantasy comes with a price that can include a defeated self-image, destruction of character, and the inability to experience true intimacy later in life. If you ignore God's design for sex in dating, you can destroy your capacity to fully enjoy it in marriage. God can renew your heart, but He rarely erases the lasting consequences that you bring upon yourself.

When we do not consciously walk in the love of Christ, we are vulnerable to dwelling upon fantasy relationships. But resisting sexual fantasy is possible when Jesus satisfies our hearts. His love is meant to fulfill us and make false relationships look foolish. It's like comparing real money to play money. Pornographic or emotional fantasies cannot offer anything close to the reality of Christ's unconditional love. When we recognize how much Jesus loves us, sexual substitutes ultimately appear unappealing and ridiculous.

How Far Is Too Far?

Now that we have covered the specifics of sexual temptation, we are back to the obvious question: How far should you go physically with your boyfriend or girlfriend? Is it okay to kiss or caress? Here is the best answer I know:

> All things are lawful for me, but not all things are profitable. All things are lawful for me, but I will not be mastered by anything.... Yet the body is not for immorality, but for the Lord, and the Lord is for the body (1 Corinthians 6:12-13).

These verses give the most insightful solution for deciding how far to go. First, verse 13 clarifies that sexual immorality is out of the question. Besides that, they advise to consider three criteria in making our decision: profitability, avoiding being mastered, and knowing that the Lord is for your body. Let's take a closer look at each.

Profitability

Choosing what is profitable in dating means making a decision that benefits or improves your relationship. As we learned in chapter 7, any type of sexual activity joins your heart to another person. The more sensual your activity together, the stronger your bond will become. However, if you break up, you will damage your hearts as you rip them apart. Does that sound very profitable?

When you bond your heart through sex to someone but don't have a commitment with that person, you take an awful risk. You would be wise to delay sensual activity until both you and the other person are committed to a lifetime together. Intense kissing or touching bonds your hearts, but you have no assurance that you will stay together. Am I saying that you should completely avoid physical contact? No, romantic touch and affection are necessary for two adults to develop intimacy. Instead, I am suggesting that you wait to kiss and touch until you are mutually pursuing a marriage commitment. Sacrificing your desires to protect each other's heart is the most profitable thing that you can do.

Avoid Being Mastered

When Paul said, "I will not be mastered by anything," he meant he avoided behavior that dominated his judgment. Certain activity, such as sexual pleasure, can become so addicting that a couple must repeat it to feel happy together. Our bodies were not wired to go backward sexually. Once we arouse our sex drive with someone, that drive is designed by God to propel us toward a complete bond in intercourse.

Therefore, if you sensually touch your boyfriend or girlfriend, you will struggle to feel satisfied with anything less. Your fleshly body will desire to intensify your involvement. Thus, if you start physical activity early in a dating relationship, you set up a long, frustrating road ahead of you. Your judgment can become clouded as sex takes control of your relationship. Eventually, your sex drive could lead you to hurry up and get married to relieve the frustration. Bear in mind that once you start *inappropriate* sensual activity, your sex drive will always want more.

The Lord Is for Your Body

First Corinthians 6:13 says, "The Lord is for the body," which indicates that God intends for Christ to live His life through you (Romans 6:13,19). You are joined to Jesus in a spiritual marriage, giving Him the ability to express His wisdom and judgment within you at all times. Since He wants the best for your dating relationships, He will never encourage physical activity until the time is right.

Don't wait, however, until you are alone with your boyfriend or girlfriend to ask Jesus what you should do. In those moments, your emotions will easily overwhelm your judgment. Instead, before you and your date get together, ask Jesus what He wants you to do. If either of you feels the least bit uneasy about any physical activity, then tell the other person that you prefer to wait—and stand by your decision.

For example, if you wonder whether kissing is appropriate for your relationship, ask Jesus with a yielded heart, "Lord, I know that You want the best for me. Would it be profitable for me to kiss my date?" If He says yes, then enjoy the moment. If He says no, then wait and thank Him for protecting you.

Jesus will tell you when moving forward physically is beneficial. How? When the time is right, He will give you and your date a *peace in your hearts.* If, however, you seek physical contact for the wrong reasons, He will convict you to slow down. Listen for His promptings.

As dating couples become mature enough to kiss responsibly, Christ will give them the freedom to enjoy it. When couples are not yet ready, Jesus will urge them to wait. If Christ wants you to wait, realize that He is not trying to steal your fun. He is working to maximize your relationship and potential enjoyment of sex in the future.

Finally, remember that if you try to control your sexual behavior by following rules, you can actually increase the likelihood that you will fall into temptation (Romans 7:7-11). Focusing on guidelines to avoid sex will wear out your self-discipline. In my dating experiences, I never had much success with my girlfriends when we set up rules to prevent touching each other. Concentrating on the rules made us think even more about kissing or caressing, and we eventually rationalized doing it. On the other hand, when I discovered that Christ is my life, my desires changed, and I sought what was best for my girlfriend. We didn't need a rule because Jesus led us to pursue what was most beneficial for our relationship.

For example, as I dated Ashley, her beauty captivated me, and Satan tempted me to dive into pleasure with her. Meanwhile, I sensed Christ's urging within my heart to wait on His timing for our first kiss. He wanted me to honor Ashley and give our relationship the best chance for maximum passion in the future. I knew from past mistakes that if we rushed into physical activity, we risked it taking over our relationship and damaging our potential for intimacy. So I asked Jesus to live His patience and self-control through me. It wasn't easy, but Ashley and I agreed that waiting was best for both of us. Then, after months of determining our compatibility and character, we eventually sensed a peaceful urge from Jesus to enjoy a good smooch together. Needless to say, our first kiss was electric. Waiting upon Christ's guidance kept us in the position to benefit from physical activity rather than be hurt by it.

If You Have Fallen

Maybe you have already fallen victim to sexual temptation. Is there still hope for you? Yes! God's love and mercy can restore your heart. However, He rarely erases your consequences. You will encounter repercussions from the sinful choices that you made. Fortunately, God promises to work the pain for your growth and benefit (Romans 8:28-29).

To begin the healing process, confess your sin to God and repent (agree with Him and turn from your inappropriate behavior). He cannot heal you until you admit a sincere desire to change your ways. As you repent, recognize that God has already forgiven you for your mistakes. You do not need to wallow in self-pity or attempt to earn His favor. In His grace and mercy, God accepts you and wants you to move toward maturity.

Next, remember that you are spiritually married to Jesus. Review all of the wonderful wedding gifts that you have as His bride (see chapter 2 for review). Realize that God has cleansed you from your transgressions and made you dead to the power of sin. Therefore, do not believe any accusations from Satan that your offenses classify you as a worthless person or a second-class Christian. God knows your faults and loves you unconditionally. Moreover, He purified your heart and gave you the righteousness of

Christ. By faith, you can allow Christ to live His holy life through you to sacrificially love other people.

If you recently made a sexual mistake, be wary of rushing into a new dating relationship. Otherwise, you could short-circuit God's healing process. Because of the consequences from your sexual sin you probably should not date for a while. Your heart needs time to mend, as may your reputation. In addition, Christ may want you to ask for forgiveness from whomever you hurt and to establish respect with that person. So be patient about your future. If you have a hard time letting go of your painful memories, you might want to seek the assistance of a Christian counselor.

Above all, remember that the love of Christ will satisfy your heart more than any sexual thrill possibly can. True fulfillment in relationships happens as He leads you to share love sacrificially rather than sexually. Through His pure passion, you can develop a dating relationship more wonderful than you ever thought possible.

Now, knowing that Jesus is your answer against premature sexual involvement, let's examine how He can protect you from a premature emotional commitment.

Personal Bible Study

1. Read Colossians 2:20-23. Why are biblical principles, willpower, or accountability groups inadequate for resisting sexual temptation?

2. What source of victory over sexual temptation is implied in Colossians 1:11 and Galatians 2:20? Does this victory have anything to do with your willpower?

3. According to Ephesians 4:17-24, how does immoral behavior originate? What is your defense against sexual immorality?

4. According to Romans 7:7-12 and 1 Corinthians 15:56, what gives sin the power to tempt you? How do you feel knowing that *you* do not cause your selfish desires?

5. Read 2 Corinthians 4:8-11, 16-17. What encouraging comments do these verses make that you can apply to your struggle against sexual temptation?

6. Are you guilty of sexual immorality in your past? Do you worry whether God still loves you? In 2 Samuel 11, King David lusted after a woman, got her pregnant, and murdered her husband to hide their affair. Meditate on the wonderful forgiveness and compassion that God extends to a repentant David in Psalm 51.

Group Discussion Questions

1. Why does sexual activity have the power to put you into bondage?

2. Identify a temptation common to everyone in your group and discuss how Christ living His life through you can effectively overcome that temptation.

3. If a guy cannot control his sexual desire with his girl-friend, what negative effect could occur if they got married?

4. Discuss why a woman who flirts continuously or wears seductive clothing might not make a good candidate for a wife.

5. What harm can pornography or steamy romance novels cause to your self-esteem and the quality of your dating relationships?

6. First Corinthians 6:12-13 says to seek profitability, avoid being mastered, and let the Lord live through your body. How can these suggestions help you determine how far to go physically in a dating relationship?

9

GUARDING
YOUR PASSION

:: :: ::

*Protecting Your Heart from
a Premature Commitment*

*J*anice dreamed of becoming a wife and mother. Yet as her dating life stagnated, she began to feel desperate. At age 29, Janice believed that time was running out. Her fears diminished, however, when she flirted at a party with a handsome man named Michael. To her delight, he asked her out to dinner at a fancy restaurant and sent roses to her office the next morning. The burst of romance swept Janice right off her feet.

The ensuing weeks progressed into a string of romantic dates and countless hours on the phone together. Janice bared her soul to Michael, relating her love for travel, desire for children, and convictions about God. Michael seemed to share similar beliefs. He even expressed his wish to get married soon and retire early to enjoy life. Janice could hardly contain her bliss as she envisioned an exciting future together.

Consequently, when Michael proposed after only five months of dating, Janice accepted without hesitation. She couldn't believe how suddenly her life had changed. All of her dreams seemed to come true as she and Michael married quickly and sped away on a honeymoon. Life seemed so full of hope and joy.

However, less than a year later, Janice's dreams began to unravel. She found herself married to a man who kept to himself, had little desire for romance, and hoarded his money. Fancy restaurants were now a wasteful indulgence, and traveling was out of the question. Janice even learned that Michael had never left the state before they met. In addition, Michael insisted that Janice postpone her desire for children and keep working to help finance his goal of early retirement. Stuck in their little house, Janice felt more like a prisoner than a wife.

Janice couldn't understand why Michael had changed. He seemed nothing like the man she had dated. Looking back, Janice wished that they had dated longer. The haste of their dating relationship had prevented her from discovering the real Michael. She found herself married to a man who did not cherish her. Quietly, Janice's heart began to die....

When you begin a new dating relationship, it is normal to feel dizzy with ecstasy. You should enjoy the thrill of romance, but you should also be aware that a romantic high can trick you into concluding that you have found a mate. As Janice found out, blissful emotions can lead you to fall in love with someone before you really know who he or she is.

Romantic emotions can blind you with misguided optimism and enthusiasm about a person when, in reality, you have little concrete knowledge about his or her integrity or maturity level. Many singles forget that in dating, people sometimes downplay their character flaws, such as arrogance, addictions, irresponsibility, or lack of faith in God.

Therefore, giving your heart to someone because of your initial impressions is risky. People can mask their imperfections to gain your acceptance. You might call it "putting your best foot forward." I am not suggesting that every person you date will misrepresent himself or herself. Just bear in mind that singles commonly conceal their faults until they win your favor. Then, once you have fallen in love, they unveil their problems. By then it is too late to change your mind without suffering heartache.

Rushing into romance is a frequent dating mistake, and this entire chapter is devoted to helping you avoid it. In the first section we will look at five major causes of a premature commitment. Then, in the second section, we will discuss ways to guard your heart. Finally, in the third section, we'll discuss how to determine the trustworthiness of the person you date.

Common Causes of a Premature Commitment

Cause #1: Dating on Potential

Ladies, have you ever dated a guy who was afraid of commitment? Did you feel tempted to crank up the romance or even offer your body to try and sway him? Guys, have you ever dated a woman you really liked, but something about her annoyed you? Maybe you wished that she would laugh more often, lose weight, or not talk so much. Did you try to cajole her into changing for you by offering promises of love?

When you consider someone as Mr. or Miss Almost Right, you wind up "dating on potential." Dating on potential is liking someone for whom you wish he or she could be rather than for whom he or she actually is. You offer your heart to someone in hopes that your "love" will remove his or her defects.

I fell into this trap when I dated my first wife. She exhibited negative behavior that concerned me. Yet rather than raising an objection or suspend our relationship, I married her, hoping my affection would encourage her to grow. Unfortunately, she never chose to deal with her problems. After seven months of marriage, those issues provoked her to abandon me.

When you date on potential, you presume that giving someone your affection can fix his or her character flaws. For example, a woman might meet a man whose integrity is questionable. Instead of guarding her heart, however, she imagines his potential and reasons that her devotion to him can help remove his faults. More often than not, though, his immaturity will dominate her life.

Character traits are complex and can take a long time to change. A dishonest man will usually struggle all of his life to tell the truth. A critical woman may never learn to appreciate the good points in other people. Likewise, a sex addict may never regain the ability to experience complete intimacy in a relationship. It is okay to urge someone to improve his or her character flaws, but as you do, keep these five points in mind:

1. People cannot improve their character unless they have an intense, internal motivation to change. You cannot make people change. They must do it because they want to themselves.

2. Only the love of Jesus Christ can truly change a person's character. Any other method is dependent upon human self-effort and offers temporary improvement at best. Furthermore, Jesus can transform a repentant person's character, but some consequences from his or her past behavior may never disappear.

3. Poor character generally takes years to improve, and the transformation is rarely easy. Be wary if a person's character seems to change overnight. He or she could be faking the change simply to gain your acceptance, or the person may be sincere but unable to make the change last.

4. If you urge your date to improve his or her character, he or she may temporarily change to appease you. However, the person will usually revert to old behaviors once he or she has your heart.

5. When you prod someone to mature, you risk that the person will become dependent upon you to make changes happen. This puts you in the awkward role of counselor, parent, or substitute for God. That role is not your responsibility. Your purpose is to encourage your date as an adult, not coddle him or her as a baby.

You can date someone and hope that he or she will mature, but committing your heart as the incentive for change is unwise. The person's lack of character could damage you. If you date a person who expresses a genuine desire to change, give him or her some leeway. Realize, however, that character improvement is a complicated, long-term process. It's better to avoid the whole problem by reserving your heart for a more mature person.

Dating someone so you can change his or her outward appearance is not a loving thing to do. Love does not coax someone to shed pounds, change hairstyles, or dress fashionably when he or she has no desire to do so. Asking someone to change for you is fine, but pressuring the person or dangling your heart in front of him or her as motivation is selfish. If you want your date to realize his or her full potential, he or she must choose to change.

Cause #2: Lack of Time Together

Some singles see no problem with giving their hearts to someone after only six months of dating. What they do not understand is how little time couples actually spend together. Allow me to walk you through a quick calculation to explain what I mean.

When couples who live in the same town date seriously, they may see each other two to four days a week. When they are on a date, they may spend an average of six hours together. Therefore, most couples only average a maximum of 24 hours per week together. Now, divide those 24 hours by 168 total hours in a week, and you discover that dating couples spend less than 15 percent of their time together! They spend the other 85 percent either alone or with other people. Worse, if two people date long-distance, they may be fortunate to spend 5 percent of their time together.

My point is that most people who are dating do not see each other as much as they may think. Furthermore, you cannot truly know someone without being face-to-face for an extended period of time. You may think quality time includes talking on the phone, communicating via Internet chat rooms, or sending e-mails, but no substitute exists for being in the same place together. Phone conversations or written correspondence cannot reveal the truth about a person's integrity, spiritual maturity, or intention to love you sacrificially. You determine these crucial qualities only by being together over a lengthy period of time.

Therefore, if you only date for a few months, you risk experiencing the same problems as Janice did in this chapter's opening story. She thought she knew Michael after only five months. In essence, she gave her heart to a stranger. Don't let the same tragedy happen to you. Date someone long enough to get beyond your initial impressions and learn the truth about that person.

Cause #3: Fantasy Hope

Michelle had had a crush on Darren since the day they met at church. Consequently, she was overjoyed when he asked her for her phone number. Immediately, Michelle began to fantasize about life as Darren's girlfriend. She daydreamed about romantic dates together, staring into his big brown eyes, and someday watching Darren propose to her with a large diamond. The more Michelle dwelled upon these blissful thoughts, the more she knew he must be The One. She could feel it inside—they were destined for each other. As she daydreamed about him, her heart fell in love. Within a matter of days, Michelle was totally convinced that Darren was her future husband. Therefore, she was crushed when he called to ask out her roommate.

Have you ever daydreamed about marrying a cute guy or girl, decided where you would live together, and determined how many children you would have—all before your first date? Daydreaming about someone is normal, but you can cross over into unrestrained fantasy and trick your heart into prematurely accepting a person. Anything your mind dwells on can lead your heart to yearn for it as a reality. Thus, the more you think about someone romantically, the stronger your desire to enter a relationship with that person. This can lead you to make dating decisions based upon emotion instead of fact. While your fantasies may feel convincing, they cannot verify the truth about someone.

Remember from chapter 6 that Satan will encourage you to look for fulfillment apart from Christ. He does this by using the flesh to make you obsess over a dating relationship. He provokes you by whispering in the first person, *It would be wonderful if I could kiss that gorgeous woman,* or *Life would be perfect if that cute guy was my boyfriend.* Satan uses fantasies to lead you to frantically pursue a man or a woman. If you listen to his lies, you can become infatuated with someone you barely know.

You can defend yourself against unbridled fantasies by keeping your thoughts rooted in the truth (see Philippians 4:8). By continually reminding yourself of the truth that Christ loves you and cares for you, you can distinguish between fact and fantasy. Furthermore, when you focus on Jesus, you can experience the peace to live one day at a time.

Cause #4: Sexual Activity

Jake met Jennifer at his health club, and her beauty captivated him. He asked her out and felt like a king when she gave him a goodnight kiss. After their second date at a concert, Jake "stumbled" upon a secluded parking spot where they could talk. An hour later, however, their bodies were doing most of the talking. The physical affection mesmerized Jake because he had never experienced such a sensation. Their third date was just as sensual, and Jake decided that he wanted to be with Jennifer forever. Consideration of her character or maturity didn't matter. All Jake knew about Jennifer was that she was beautiful and a great kisser. Their hot romance convinced him to blindly give her his heart. Thus, he was devastated when she suddenly dumped him two months later for a different guy at their health club.

Nothing confuses a dating decision as much as sexual activity. The moment you begin to romantically touch someone, your heart will feel a desire to bond with that person. That's because God created sex to join two people together. Sexual involvement leads your heart to want more (see chapter 8 for review).

Therefore, when you kiss or touch someone, you hasten your desire to commit to that person. This means that you overlook such important factors as character, spiritual maturity,

and sacrificial love. Premarital sexual activity clouds your judgment and urges you to rush ahead for more pleasure. That urge
overshadows your concern about a person's integrity, communication skills, or spiritual depth. Furthermore, if you have intercourse with someone, you bond your body and soul to that person
whether or not he or she is right for you (1 Corinthians 6:16).
Should you break that bond, you will suffer painful consequences.

If you are sexually involved with someone, consider the risk
that you are taking. Physical affection may feel good, but it can
numb you to what your heart really wants—someone trustworthy, kind, and willing to sacrifice for you. Think about what is
best for the long run.

Jesus does not want you to cheat yourself over temporary
sexual pleasure. Instead, He wants the best for you. If you allow sex
to govern your relationship, you practically ensure that you will
commit your heart too soon.

Cause #5: A Starving Heart

The most common reason why singles prematurely give
their hearts away originates from a deep hunger to be accepted.
Your heart needs love just as your body needs food, and when
your heart is starving, it can drive you to seek a serious relationship simply to feel better. Consider the analogy of a man starving
for food. In desperation, his appetite can convince him to eat anything—even something that might be poisonous. Likewise, if you
desperately seek acceptance, your hungry heart can persuade you
to jump into a romantic relationship even if it is unhealthy.

If Jesus is not your primary Source of love, your heart will
chase acceptance elsewhere, especially when you feel lonely. At
these times, a dating relationship may look like the perfect solution. However, the problem with trying to feed your heart with
romance is that human love is performance based. You must keep
your date happy to maintain his or her affection. Yet keeping
someone constantly happy is impossible, and the disappointment

or conflict that results will prevent your relationship from fulfilling you.

Like eating chocolate, dating is meant to be a fun part of life. Yet just as chocolate cannot keep your body alive, a boyfriend or girlfriend cannot fulfill your heart's need for unconditional love. God intends to satisfy your heart with the love that you already have from Christ. Dating simply gives you the opportunity to share His love with someone else.

Guarding Your Heart from Falling Too Soon

Now that we know why people fall in love too quickly, let's look at several ways to protect your heart when it seems to be melting. You can guard yourself by dating until you determine consistency, keeping your options open, and, best of all, living in the love of Christ.

Date Until You Determine Consistency

After a few dates you might assume that you know someone, but you have only just begun. In several of my relationships, I mistakenly believed the adage "what you see is what you get." In dating, however, you cannot rely on that phrase. People tend to conceal their imperfections as long as possible. As a result, someone may seem sweet and honest when you first meet, but that may not be his or her true disposition.

When you begin a new relationship, reserve your affection until you determine what is *consistent* about that person. This realistic approach blocks your emotions from taking control. Restrain your heart until you spend time together over many months. This doesn't mean that you can't like the other person or have fun dating each other. Neither am I suggesting that you create a stoic or unromantic relationship. On the contrary, dating should be exciting. Yet you can make the clear decision to have fun with someone while simultaneously holding your heart in check.

Dating to determine consistency gives you the advantage of discovering how a person acts in various situations over a long period of time. This insight is valuable because if you get engaged to someone, you want a good idea of how that person will treat you as a spouse. Most singles can generate courtesy on a first date after a stressful day at work. But you want to know if he or she will continue to be polite under stressful situations should you get married. The best way to predict how a person might behave later in your relationship is to date him or her long enough to determine their normal conduct.

Establishing consistency does not mean looking for someone who is dull or predictable. It is the process of determining an accurate picture of the person you date. As you spend time together, ask yourself questions such as these:

- Does the person voice his or her convictions and stick to them?
- Does the person maintain faith in God during bad circumstances?
- Does the person exhibit unpredictable or drastic mood swings?
- Does the person generally accept you or criticize you?
- Does the person's behavior change considerably when he or she gets angry or depressed?

Determining consistency clarifies whether the attributes you like about another person will remain in your relationship. This can apply to both internal and external characteristics. For example, if a woman appreciates that her new boyfriend is considerate and prompt, she needs to make sure that he is consistent in that area. Most guys know that they should be punctual and polite when they initially date a woman. However, give most men a few months, and they tend to slack a little on their manners. Similarly, if a guy likes a certain woman because she eats healthy food and exercises regularly, he needs to date her long enough to determine whether that is her normal lifestyle or just a passing fad.

As you date, also notice whether the things that are important to you are important to your boyfriend or girlfriend. Does the person place a similar priority on the values, ideas, and preferences that are significant to you? For instance, ladies, if you enjoy long talks about deep subjects, does your boyfriend consistently want to join you? Guys, if you believe that hanging out with your buddies is important, is your girlfriend cooperative? In addition, does the person you date share a consistent desire to grow spiritually? If something is a priority for you, you need to date long enough to make sure that it is a priority for the other person. Otherwise, you will live at odds over crucial issues should you get married.

How long does it take to determine consistency about someone? Long enough to confirm how someone behaves in both good and bad times. Don't get serious with someone on a hunch. Date long enough to develop proof. If you date a longtime family friend, you may need less than a year to feel convinced. On the other hand, if you recently met someone, it would be wise to date for a year or longer to confirm consistency. Also, listen to your friends or family. If they feel that you are moving too fast, then slow down because their point of view is usually more objective. There is no harm in waiting a little longer to make a wise dating decision. Like Janice, if you date and marry in haste, you could one day wake up wondering, "Who is this person?"

Keep Your Options Open

If you have a dating history of committing your heart too quickly, here is a practical way to guard yourself. At the start of a new relationship, politely mention that you wish to remain free to date other people. You could say, "I enjoy going out with you, but let's maintain our freedom until we've had more time to get to know each other." By doing so, you keep your relational options open until you can determine whether that person has character.

This plan not only prevents you from giving away your heart too quickly but also maintains your focus on discerning the person's integrity.

Keeping your dating options open is a fair request in a new relationship. If the other person objects, he or she may selfishly intend to date you to meet his or her needs. Remember that throughout the entire dating process, including engagement, you are free. Therefore, do not let someone pressure you into making a commitment. Consider dating exclusively once you have spent several months together and confirmed that person's character. No one but you has control over your heart.

Live in the Love of Christ

The best way to guard your heart against a premature commitment is to recognize that Jesus offers you all of the love you need. As we have discussed, you have amazing worth in Christ's eyes. His passion for you is unconditional, and you will never find a boyfriend or a girlfriend who will love you as deeply as He does. When you experience Christ's love, the romantic approval of a man or a woman becomes less important. You have no reason to obsess over a dating relationship when the Lord of the universe thinks that you are wonderful.

Furthermore, the love of Jesus does not make human relationships irrelevant. Romance and human affection are good. However, Jesus does not want dating to control your life. He wants His love to control your dating decisions (2 Corinthians 5:14).

Jesus is a romantic Person, and He wants to love others through you. At the same time, He wants to protect your heart by creating the desires within you to date someone. When you follow His urging, you will know when to get involved with someone and when to separate.

We learned in chapter 4 that Christ's presence within your heart can take much of the confusion out of dating. He says, "My grace is sufficient for you, for power is perfected in weakness" (2 Corinthians 12:9). By His grace, Christ volunteers His wisdom to your finite, human mind. He does this by prompting within you the direction you should take. He gives you the desire to move forward or wait on a relationship. This is what the apostle Paul meant when he prayed

> that He [the Father] would grant you, according to the riches of His glory, to be strengthened with power through His Spirit in the inner man (Ephesians 3:16).

The love of Christ is the best protection against going overboard emotionally. He can keep your heart in check by urging you to maintain a realistic perspective about someone. In addition, Jesus will lead you to seek what is beneficial for you and your date. He will give you wisdom to know when to withdraw from a bad relationship or pursue a good relationship further. As you listen and yield to Christ, His grace will be sufficient to meet all of your needs—including your dating decisions.

Determining Trustworthiness in Dating

Entrusting your heart to someone is a serious matter because some singles will not date you with good intentions. Therefore, do not flippantly decide to trust a person. A prospective marriage partner needs to earn your trust. I know of at least four ways to assess a person's trustworthiness. These include asking questions about your date's character, considering your date's family and friends, seeking pre-engagement counseling, and listening to the Holy Spirit. Use all four approaches to maximize your judgment. The more you know about someone, the more confidently you can trust him or her.

Ask Questions About Your Date's Character

Dating is similar to a job search because it is an interview process. You are spending time with someone to discover your compatibility. Simply being together, however, does not provide you with the necessary information to build trust. If you want to determine someone's trustworthiness, you need to promote conversation that has depth. This involves asking questions about someone's convictions, past experiences, spiritual beliefs, and relationship history. Discussing these topics may not sound romantic or fun, but it is crucial to learning to trust your date.

Examining someone's character does not have to be an uncomfortable process if you use tact and diplomacy. The key is to establish chemistry with a person before you ask about personal issues. For instance, you probably should not ask on a first or second date whether the person has had sex or tried illegal drugs. Rushing into an interrogation could give your date the wrong impression and scare him or her off. Instead, wait to ask character questions after you have developed some rapport together.

In addition, show sympathy and discretion when you probe into someone's personal mistakes. By asking questions appropriately, you demonstrate compassion and interest. Your goal is not to try and set someone straight but to learn what a person believes and whether he or she follows those convictions. To get you started, see pages 179-180 for a list of character questions. I recommend that you address every question on this list before you consider engagement.

In addition, when you ask your date a question, do not settle for superficial or pat answers. Sometimes the best questions include "Could you clarify that for me?" or "Could you tell me more?" Remember Janice? She asked Michael whether he liked to travel but forgot to clarify the places he had actually visited. In truth, Michael had never left the state prior to meeting Janice, but she didn't discover this fact until after they married. Janice settled for a shallow answer and got burned. That's why brief responses or one-word answers do not help when you are exploring someone's beliefs, past, or integrity. The depth of your communication greatly determines the quality of your relationship, and shallow answers usually indicate a shallow person.

Assessing a person's character includes observing whether your date's behavior matches what he or she says. Trust actions more than words (1 John 3:18). For instance, if your girlfriend promises to do something, does she follow through on it? If your boyfriend claims that he is a Christian, does he yield his desires to Christ? If your date says that he or she wants to make a difference in people's lives, does he or she consistently show kindness, generosity, or encouragement to others? Basically, does your date walk the talk? To establish trust with someone, you need factual evidence of a person's behavior over time.

Consider Your Date's Family and Friends

Never underestimate the value of visiting with your date's family to gain insight into his or her character. If you get to meet the parents, use that opportunity to observe how your date interacts with them. If your date's family cannot trust their son or daughter, you probably cannot either.

Family relationships are one of the biggest influences on a person's character. *Remember that if you marry someone, you will also marry his or her family.* If you detect relational problems in the person's family, discuss them because those problems will likely affect your relationship. In addition, ladies, watch how your boyfriend gets along with his mother. Are they close and supportive or indifferent toward each other? Guys, notice whether your girlfriend has a loving relationship with her father. Are they affectionate and respectful, or do they avoid one another?

Your date's friends reflect his or her character as well. Does your boyfriend or girlfriend hang around people who are genuine or dishonest? Ladies, consider whether people respect your boyfriend. What is his reputation among his peers? Guys, does your girlfriend get along with her friends? Are people wary around her because she likes to gossip? Does she have any girlfriends, or does she mostly hang out with guys? The answers to these questions can reveal character defects that can damage your relationship. If the person you date does not have any friends, then you have a clear sign of relational immaturity.

Generally, your date will treat you just as he or she treats others. Therefore, when you participate in a group activity together, watch how he or she acts. Is he or she bossy, sarcastic, critical, mean, or stoic, or is he or she polite, cooperative, accepting, honest, and loyal? The way a person behaves in public reveals his or her trustworthiness.

Seek Pre-engagement Counseling

Before you decide to trust someone with your heart in marriage, seek pre-engagement counseling. Why? *Once the engagement ring sits on a woman's finger, you can lose much of your objectivity about a relationship.* Likewise, when you are engaged, the priority of your relationship becomes your wedding day. This can make it nearly impossible to stop and deal with any character flaws that you discover. Furthermore, the embarrassment of calling off a wedding can deter you from being honest about character traits that bother you. Engagement tends to make you ignore problems and push them into marriage, where they wreak havoc.

To avoid this dilemma, visit a trained Christian counselor who can help you examine all aspects of your relationship. A counselor can ask the important character questions that you may have forgotten. Best of all, a pre-engagement counselor can detect problem areas that could damage your future together. Going for counseling does not mean that anything is wrong with your relationship. Neither does it mean that you have to marry the person you are dating. Instead, counseling examines the critical aspects of your relationship to make sure that your boyfriend or girlfriend is right for you.

When looking for a counselor, attempt to find a Christian trained to deal with marriage and relational issues. Many people may offer to counsel you, but if they do not have adequate training, they may not be able to effectively handle the problem areas of your relationship. If you cannot find a qualified counselor, visit the websites for Focus on the Family (www.fotf.org) or the

American Association of Christian Counselors (www.aacc.net) for information about counseling services in your area.

A pre-engagement counselor will usually spend four to ten sessions with you and your date. Prepare to discuss key areas of your relationship, including personality differences, family and child issues, past relationships, spiritual maturity, financial issues, and sexual expectations. Most importantly, the counselor should review the truths of Christ's unconditional love to make sure you understand how it applies to your relationship. Honesty is crucial when you meet with a counselor. If something concerns you or your date, the private counseling session is a good place to bring it up.

After dating Ashley for many months, I arranged for us to visit a licensed Christian counselor through a program at our church. Over a period of eight weeks, the counselor examined our relationship in such areas as finances, family concerns, personality differences, spiritual understanding and sexual expectations. The counseling sessions were not always fun, but the discussions gave Ashley and me a sense of confidence about pursuing marriage. The process also got our families more involved in our relationship and helped give them a peace about our future. Overall, the counseling was invaluable because it reinforced our compatibility and intensified my desire to truly love Ashley. Shortly thereafter, I joyfully proposed to her on a mountaintop on July 4, 1999.

Investing in pre-engagement counseling is worth the time and money because it helps you determine whether you should entrust your heart to your boyfriend or girlfriend. By sharing your relationship with a wise and objective third party, you can gain the assurance necessary to move confidently toward a lifelong commitment.

Listen to the Holy Spirit

The final step in discerning whether you can trust someone is to listen to the Holy Spirit. Through the Holy Spirit, Jesus resides within you to be your primary source of relational wisdom. His discernment can help you determine someone's character.

> But you have received the Holy Spirit, and he lives within
> you, so you don't need anyone to teach you what is true.
> For the Spirit teaches you all things, and what he teaches
> is true—it is not a lie. So continue in what he has taught
> you, and continue to live in Christ (1 John 2:27 NLT).

When you yield yourself to Christ, He can impart to you a sense of peace or concern about your relationship. One way to sense His discernment is by asking yourself, *Do I feel safe when I am with my date?* By safe, I'm not referring to physical protection. I'm talking about a feeling deep within you. When you are quiet and honest with yourself, do you sense a prevailing peace about this person, or do you have any definable apprehension or hesitancy about your future together? Jesus can guide your heart through the Holy Spirit when you surrender to Him.

Maybe you have dated someone for several years but still lack a peace about getting married. That could be Jesus telling you to stop dating just for companionship. Either move toward intimacy or break up. If you feel a distinct fear about trusting someone, maybe he or she is too immature, or maybe you are demanding perfection. Listen to the Holy Spirit. If He convicts you, then let Him direct your decision.

Christ has your best interests in mind, and He will not lead you astray. He will inform you when you can safely trust someone. Above all, Jesus wants you to trust in Him. His passionate love not only protects your heart but also empowers you to detect issues that could sabotage your dating relationship.

31 Character Questions

Fully discuss each of these questions before you consider engagement. (Remember to develop rapport before talking about these intimate issues.)

Spiritual Character

- Who is Jesus Christ to you?
- When and how did you become a Christian?
- What is your spiritual gift?
- Are you involved in a local church or Bible study?

Financial Character

- Do you have any debt? If so, how much?
- If you have debt, how long will it take you to get rid of it?
- Do you have a stable employment history?
- How much do you have in a savings account? Retirement account?
- Do you consistently give money to the church or to the less fortunate?

Dating Character

- Tell me about your past dating relationships.
- Are you still involved in any other relationships?
- Have you ever been engaged? If yes, why was it called off?
- Have you been divorced? If yes, why did your marriage fail? Any children?

Sexual Character

- Are you comfortable waiting for sex until marriage?
- Have you ever had sex? If yes, how recently?
- Are you carrying any sexually transmitted diseases?
- Have you ever struggled with homosexuality?
- Have you ever had an abortion?

General Character

- What difficult circumstances have you endured?
- What makes you passionate in life?
- Have you ever broken the law?
- In what ways are you involved in helping others?

Friends and Family

- Who are your friends?
- Do you get along well with your family? Why or why not?
- Is your family excited about our relationship?
- What are your views about the roles of a husband and wife?
- Do you want to have children if you get married? How many? How soon?

Addictions

- Are you addicted to alcohol, substances, pornography, or anything else?
- Have you ever smoked, used drugs, or struggled with an eating disorder?
- Do you have family members who wrestle with addictions?
- Do you gamble or play the lottery?

Personal Bible Study

1. What eight types of thoughts does Philippians 4:7-8 recommend that you dwell on? How can these thoughts guard your heart against unrealistic fantasies or a premature commitment?

2. Read 2 Thessalonians 3:3-5. What protection do these verses suggest against falling in love too quickly?

3. According to 1 Thessalonians 3:12-13, how does love originate within you? Who is responsible for keeping your heart blameless?

4. How is trustworthy behavior identified in 1 John 2:4-6?

5. Read James 1:19-27. What kind of conduct should you expect from the person you date?

6. How does Proverbs 13:10 apply to the decision to date someone seriously?

Group Discussion Questions

1. Why is dating someone for the purpose of changing him or her an unloving thing to do? Also, why is dating someone in hopes that the person's character will improve a risky move?

2. Discuss why physical activity can fool your heart into prematurely falling in love with someone.

3. Name two advantages of dating to determine consistent behavior in someone before giving that person your heart.

4. Why is the love of Christ the best protection against going overboard emotionally in a dating relationship?

5. What are the benefits of having a Christian counselor help you examine your dating relationship before you get engaged? Can anyone in your group recommend a good pre-engagement Christian counselor?

6. How does meeting your boyfriend or girlfriend's family and friends offer insight into that person's character and ability to love you?

10

THE SABOTAGE
OF PASSION

:: :: ::

*Recognizing the Baggage
That Destroys Relationships*

urt had dated Stephanie for nine months. He was enamored
with her wit, beauty, and intelligence, and he attempted to dazzle
her with extravagant gifts. Stephanie relished being treated like a
queen and was amazed at how successful and generous Curt
appeared. Consequently, she was puzzled one evening when she
accidentally overheard Curt arguing on the phone with a collec-
tions agency. He was late on a loan payment of more than $5000.
Stephanie immediately confronted Curt, and he was forced to
reveal the truth.

All his life, Curt had believed the lie that he needed to impress
others by appearing wealthy. To keep up his well-to-do image, he
took out huge loans on a fancy sports car and a large house. In
addition, he used his credit cards to buy lavish toys and vacation
getaways. Eventually, his income could not keep up with his
spending, and he wound up more than $45,000 in debt.

Stephanie was shocked at the reality of Curt's overwhelming
financial situation. Soon after, she chose to end their relationship so that his debt would not become her burden. He begged

her to stay, but his dishonesty about the matter had broken their trust. Furthermore, Stephanie no longer believed that Curt was mature enough to provide stability in a marriage. His spending habits were out of control. He had secretly hoped that Stephanie's good job and fiscal maturity would save him from his financial mess.

Curt's misuse of money is just one example of how Satan uses the sinful flesh to persuade people to indulge their selfish interests. In chapter 6, we discussed that whenever Christians try to fulfill their needs apart from Jesus Christ, they sin by walking after the flesh. Worse, when people allow the flesh to control their behavior, they accumulate unwanted "baggage."

Baggage results when a person believes that a substance, person, or possession can fulfill his or her life more than Christ can. Obvious examples of baggage include an addiction to drugs, alcohol, or sex. However, financial debt, immature dependence upon parents, and a craving for acceptance also qualify as baggage. Everyone, including Christians, can carry baggage. No one is immune to it. To get rid of it, we have to uncover the lies behind the problems. Otherwise, baggage will dominate a dating relationship.

Many singles attempt to hide their baggage when they are desperate for approval. Thus, it is important to learn how to detect the symptoms and negative effects that baggage can cause. This chapter will discuss nine common types of baggage that can harm dating relationships. *My list is by no means exhaustive.* The flesh can produce thousands of different relational problems within people. Therefore, ask the Holy Spirit to alert you if your date struggles with any of the issues we discuss or any other issues not mentioned here.

As you read this chapter, you may realize that you carry baggage from your past. If so, do not assume that you can ignore the problem or confront it on your own. Many types of baggage are so detrimental that you may need the assistance of a trained Christian counselor to remove them. We will discuss how to confront baggage issues and the benefits of counseling in the last part of this chapter.

Common Relational Baggage in Dating

Baggage Issue #1: Financial Debt

As we saw with Curt, many singles fall prey to using money or material things to improve their personal image. Others succumb to buying whatever they want whenever they want it. Still other singles may not generate any debt, but their overspending can leave them with nothing in savings. Any of these financial problems can damage a relationship.

Debt and the misuse of money reveal an overall attitude of impatience or desire for immediate gratification. In addition, many people who amass large consumer debt (more than $5000) have an unrealistic view of the future. Rather than create a plan to manage their money, they blindly assume that things will somehow work out. These beliefs result from falling for the lie that possessions will satisfy more than the love of Christ will. When debt dictates a lifestyle, it produces financial bondage. The consequences that result have the power to control the individual's life as well as the life of anyone he or she dates.

Repercussions from poorly managed finances can include personal bankruptcy, repossession of homes or cars, immense stress from handling creditors, and the inability to provide for a family. Debt or the lack of savings also puts a person and his or her loved ones in jeopardy of losing everything should a major illness, job loss, or car breakdown suddenly occur.

Surprisingly, many singles are reluctant to question their date's financial status. They don't want to appear nosy. Nevertheless, this information is vital to the well-being of a relationship. Therefore, once a couple entertains the prospect of marriage, it is important that they gain a clear picture of each other's financial health. The following seven questions can help to begin the discussion:

• Do you have any debt? If so, how much and why?

- What consistent actions are you taking to reduce the debt?
- When do you reasonably expect all of the debt to be paid off?
- What is your current income? How long has it been at that level?
- Do you have a detailed budget?
- How much money do you have in savings and retirement accounts?
- Do you have a steady employment history?

If your boyfriend or girlfriend refuses to openly answer these questions with you, I recommend suspending your relationship. Most likely, he or she is hiding negative information, and you do not want to become shackled to the problem. If he or she admits to having debt, do not casually dismiss it as something that will soon disappear. It is wise not to proceed toward marriage until the person can provide evidence that he or she is removing the debt.

Debt and a need for material possessions are usually symptoms of a spiritual problem. The root issue is a belief in the fleshly lie that having stuff will quench your thirst for happiness. If you or the person you date struggles with overspending, ask Christ for His self-control to design a budget and stick with it. His life within you is the ultimate Source of financial wisdom.

Understand that experiencing freedom from financial bondage can take several years. Seeking counsel from a professional financial advisor may be necessary. Check out the websites of Crown Financial Ministries (www.crown.org) or Dave Ramsey (www.daveramsey.com) for resources that offer help with debt counseling and other money matters.

Above all, do not ignore your debt. The stress from financial problems is one of the most common causes of divorce. Therefore, avoid dating or marrying someone until you can enjoy a debt-free relationship.

Baggage Issue #2: Addictions

Christians are most content when the love of Jesus Christ satisfies them. Satan uses the flesh, however, to urge you to depend upon fulfillment through people, substances, or possessions. When you think of addictions, you might list smoking, alcoholism, drug use, eating disorders, gambling, and sexual addictions. Yet people can also develop obsessions to the Internet, shopping, exercise, a career, or a hobby. Satan will try anything to put you in bondage.

An addiction occurs when a person depends on something in order to function. This bondage can result from dependence on a substance, person, or activity, and addictive behavior is rarely limited to just one thing. Addicts continually believe the lies of the flesh, so if they believe one lie, they will usually believe several. For example, a woman addicted to alcohol may quit for a while and find herself hooked on shopping or overeating. Likewise, a man may rotate between addictions to pornography, gambling, or working late. If the man does not let Christ alone satisfy him, the flesh can steer him from one harmful habit to another.

Some addictions, such as alcoholism or gambling, may begin innocently as a person drinks socially or bets on a sporting event with friends. But as a person repeats the activity, he or she begins to develop a dependence upon the good feeling. This may cause some people to deny their obsession because it developed so gradually that they do not realize they have a problem.

Others wrestle with a dependency for so long that they resign themselves to failure. Their lives become sad attempts to hide their habits. This means that many people learn to skillfully conceal their vices. Therefore, when you date someone, watch for signs that could indicate an addiction, such as the inability to delay gratification, denial of a problem, claims that he or she can quit voluntarily, refusal to discuss certain topics, deteriorating health, chronic fatigue, anger, or anxiety.

Human willpower is not strong enough to overcome an addiction. If you have a dangerous habit or suspect that your boyfriend or girlfriend does, please take it seriously. I suggest putting your relationship on hold and seeking help immediately. Then wait until you see a proven track record of freedom from the addiction before you date any further.

Only faith in the unconditional love of Jesus Christ can completely break an addiction. Medication or willpower provide short-term solutions, but victory comes when a person replaces his or her obsession with a dependence upon Christ for fulfillment in life (1 Corinthians 6:9-11; Ephesians 2:3-6). Many times, though, people need Christian counseling to apply these truths. See the end of this chapter for more information about how counseling can help a person overcome an addiction.

Baggage Issue #3: Divorce

Divorce is so rampant in our society that you might date someone who has been married before. Speaking from experience, I encourage you to move slowly. The heartache, depression, and disappointment of divorce can scar a person for a long time. Resist the urge, however, to reject every divorced person you meet. Some of them did not want their divorces; their spouses deserted them. New laws allow for immature people to easily abandon their marriages, and loving spouses have little power to stop them.

In his book *What God Wishes Christians Knew About Christianity*, Bill Gillham emphasizes the difference between a divorcé (or divorcée) and a divorcer. Divorcé's are not willing participants in a divorce. They do everything within their power to dissuade but are victimized by a divorcer's actions.[1] A divorcé never wanted his or her previous marriage to end and was committed to keeping it together. However, divorcés are not perfect or baggage free. The pain and shock from their broken marriages may still require healing. Yet a divorcé recognizes the sanctity of a marriage commitment and desires to make it last.

On the other hand, Bill Gillham describes divorcers as instigators of a biblically unjustified act against God, their spouse, and their family. A biblically unjustified divorce happens when someone leaves the marriage "merely because one is unhappy, weary of the relationship, or has found a new love, etc."[2] Divorcers seek convenience and refuse to respect their commitments. If times get hard or they become unhappy, they rationalize ending their relationships. A divorcer poses a risk because if he or she has left someone once, what will stop him or her from leaving you? Divorcers' past actions prove that their promises may be secondary to their happiness.

If you date a divorced person, please realize what you face. I suggest that you attempt to determine whether he or she is a divorcer or divorcé. To find out, you will have to dig for the real causes of the divorce. If you need any help working through your concerns, visit a Christian counselor together to discuss the issue.

Realize that a divorced person could be carrying baggage issues, such as physical abuse, child custody issues, low self-esteem, sexual dysfunction, or fear of commitment. Make sure the person has resolved those issues before you give him or her your heart.

Baggage Issue #4: Dating on the Rebound

Tom always had a girlfriend. He couldn't remember the last time he had sat home alone on a weekend. He constantly dated to maintain his self-esteem. However, his four-month-old relationship with Renee didn't work out, and he found himself lonely on a Saturday night. So he did the one thing he thought would help him feel better. He pulled out his address book and began to call every girl he knew.

After leaving messages for several girls, Tom's spirits rose when Olivia answered the phone. "Hey, Olivia, it's me, Tom. What are you doing this evening?"

"Not much," she replied. "I'm surprised to hear your voice."

Optimistic, Tom asked, "Sounds like you're available. Would you be interested in going to a movie tonight?"

"No, Tom," Olivia said, "I'm sitting here talking with Renee, your ex-girlfriend of two days. Goodbye, Mr. Desperate."

Tom was busted.

Many singles cannot stand to be alone because they believe the lie that they are incomplete without a boyfriend or girlfriend. So if they lose a relationship, their self-esteem disappears with it. Quickly, they hunt for another relationship to restore their significance. Sometimes people call this dating on the rebound. When someone is on the rebound, he or she harbors the pain and rejection from a previous relationship. The person feels a need to date someone else to ease the heartache. People on the rebound forget that Jesus wants to comfort them during their trials.

Beware of rebounders because their goal is not to love you. Instead, they want you to feed their hungry heart, and they will resort to manipulation to trick you into accepting them. They might charm you with such tactics as flattery, smothering, flirting, or trying to get pity.

How do you detect rebounders and guard against them using you? Before you start dating someone new, ask the person how long his or her previous relationship lasted and when it ended. If the person seriously dated someone within the past six months, his or her heart may still feel broken. If the last relationship ended less than three months ago, be very careful because that person could be rebounding. His or her interest in dating may be an attempt to draw fulfillment out of you.

Only time and the unconditional love of Christ can heal a broken heart. Therefore, avoid romance with someone until you are sure he or she has healed from the last relationship. Popular psychology may suggest overcoming a broken heart by dating again as soon as possible. This is bad advice, however, because it encourages people to draw their self-esteem from the approval of other people.

You can tell whether someone has healed from a past relationship by whether he or she feels peaceful and content to not date anyone. In other words, the person is open to dating but doesn't need to. Emotional healing is important because anyone who experiences rejection needs time without distraction to be reminded of Christ's complete acceptance.

Baggage Issue #5: Detrimental Sexual Experiences

Tracy was a young girl when her father sexually abused her. His awful actions convinced her that she was only lovable if she gave her body to a man. So when she dated, she offered sex to men, hoping they would give her the true love that her father withheld. Tracy believed that she had to entice men with sensuality to secure the love she craved. However, the more she used her body to keep a man interested, the less sex seemed to satisfy. Even when she had influence over a relationship, Tracy still felt more like an object than a person.

Sexual abuse is one of the most tragic types of relational baggage. When innocent children and teens are molested, their self-esteem is crushed. In addition, problems such as the inability to trust, fear of intimacy, constant feelings of being a victim, or the need to control others can wreak havoc in their adult lives. Thus, if you or someone you date has been abused, please seek Christian counseling to replace the memories of hurt with the reality of God's love.

Other types of sexual baggage include abortion, sexually transmitted diseases, unwanted pregnancy, damaged reputation, and the inability to keep commitments. These consequences result when someone engages in sex for his or her personal pleasure. Therefore, you would be wise to uncover your date's sexual history before your relationship becomes serious.

Satan commonly uses sex to create a stronghold in a person's mind. A stronghold occurs when someone allows sinful lies to control their choices. This means that once a person has participated in inappropriate sexual experiences, he or she can more easily fall prey to that temptation again.

If you or your date had sex in a previous relationship, I urge you to take your current relationship slowly and postpone physical contact. Date long enough to determine if you have both learned to rely upon Christ for His self-control. If you cannot exhibit modesty and self-restraint, then you are not ready to date.

A more subtle form of sexual baggage manifests itself as sensual behavior. Sensuality stems from an ignorance or unwillingness to receive Christ's unconditional love. People act sensually when they attempt to find acceptance by using their bodies or language to command the attention of others. They do this through seductive clothing, sexual teasing, or lewd, flirtatious remarks. For example, a woman who consistently dresses scantily is signaling a desperate need for men to accept her. She is willing to ruin her reputation to get attention. It is fine for someone to accentuate his or her attractiveness, but teasing others with appearance or words is a selfish gesture.

Baggage Issue #6: Lack of Same-Sex Friends

When a woman cannot develop close friendships with other women, she might have character problems. This baggage issue also applies to men. A lack of same-sex friends can indicate that a person is difficult to get along with. Or it could mean that others of the same sex do not respect him or her. For example, a woman who gauges her acceptability by the praise of men may view another woman as a threat to her self-esteem. She will be catty or antagonistic around other women and prevent good relationships from forming with them. Men can suffer a similar problem. If they cannot garner the respect of other men, they may spend their time with women to boost their self-esteem. The root of these problems is a misguided belief that the opposite sex, rather than Jesus Christ, can fulfill the need for unconditional love.

If you discover that the person you are dating has no same-sex friends (or no friends at all!), be cautious about continuing your relationship. Bring the problem to the person's attention and encourage him or her to develop these important friendships. You might even do some activities together in groups to help foster new friendships.

Close friends of the same sex are essential to a person's relational health. Men and women need time with others of their gender, doing things that the opposite sex might not enjoy as much. God made men and women different, and we need time to express ourselves in ways that the opposite sex may not appreciate. You will not mature as God intends if you do not spend regular time with same-sex friends. So encourage your dating partner to do activities with his or her friends apart from you.

Baggage Issue #7: Premature Trust

After dating Rick for six months, Donna really enjoyed their close friendship and deep, intellectual discussions. However, Rick began to repeatedly pressure Donna about getting married, which made her feel nervous. She liked Rick but had concerns about their contrasting careers and his ability to provide for a family. Rick worked two part-time jobs, had no insurance, and seemed content to live on a limited income. Meanwhile, Donna had a well-paying corporate job but hoped to stop working and start a family.

Whenever Donna mentioned the disparity in their careers or ideas about the future, Rick insisted that their love could overcome their differences. In addition, he asserted that God would somehow work everything out. The longer they dated, the more he pushed Donna to consider marriage. He would say, "We've dated for more than six months now. I love you and totally trust you. Why can't you trust me enough to get engaged?" Donna felt uneasy every time he asked that question.

Some singles carry the baggage of premature trust. They tend to quickly fall in love and expect others to trust them implicitly. They make pointed comments, such as "I trust you. Why can't you trust me?" This question may sound innocent, but self-seeking motives are behind it.

Other people must earn your trust. It is completely normal if you need a lot of time before you can trust someone. You develop confidence in a person through observing consistent behavior.

So if someone prematurely asks you to trust him or her, be suspicious and date that person with caution. Singles who expect blind faith are either looking to take advantage of you or hiding something negative. In some instances, a guy will pressure a girl to trust him so that he can exploit her sexually.

Premature trust can also occur when someone says "I love you" soon after a new dating relationship begins. Save this important phrase until you establish a mutual trust with someone. If a person hastily concludes that someone is perfect for him or her, the person is usually not in love. Instead, he or she has been deluded by infatuation. True love takes time to develop. Therefore, someone would be foolish to say "I love you" before he or she has taken the time to get to know you.

Other singles may prematurely say "I love you" as a ploy to push their relationships to a deeper romantic level. If you do not guard your heart, you can fall for this tactic because the emotional praise feels good. Yet true love involves a willingness to sacrifice for someone. If someone pressures you to trust him or her romantically but won't sacrifice his or her desires for your benefit, then consider the person's words empty. Leave that person and reserve your heart for someone who is willing to earn your trust.

Baggage Issue #8: Dependence on Family Members

Tina enjoyed dating her new boyfriend, Ray, until something strange happened one evening. They were watching TV at Ray's apartment when someone knocked at the door. Tina answered and was shocked when Ray's mother entered with a load of clean, neatly folded laundry for him. After unloading his clothes, Ray's mother chatted with him about his week and then slipped some cash into his wallet. Tina cringed in disbelief. Ray was 27 years old and still dependent upon his mother.

Some single adults rely too much on their parents. They childishly look to Mom or Dad for financial support, relational advice, or emotional support. Unfortunately, some parents exacerbate the problem because they draw their self-worth from their children. To feel valued, a mother or father may wrongly encourage an adult child to depend upon him or her. For instance, some singles living at home still allow their parents to do all of their laundry, clean their room, buy their groceries, and pay their bills. These singles become spoiled and never learn how to take care of themselves.

If you date someone who depends on his or her parents too much, watch out. Your date's behavior can ruin your relationship. In his book *Finding the Love of Your Life*, Dr. Neil Clark Warren explains that "some people will feel a need to run home or be on the phone with Mom or Dad frequently to ask advice. Or they will always worry that they must make decisions in just the way Dad or Mom want[s] them to. This leaves their mate feeling like he or she has married a committee rather than an individual."[3] People can have such strong emotional or financial ties to their parents that they cannot break away.

If parents get too involved in your dating or marital life, they can destroy your relationships. Therefore, you need to examine whether you and your date have appropriately broken away from your parents. Dr. Warren clarifies that a proper separation from parents means relationships in which we are "emotionally independent individuals—so we do not have to make decisions and live our lives to please them...and, we have established a relationship with our parents in which they will not intrude, dictate in any authoritative ways, and yet we can still maintain a closeness and connectedness to them."[4]

Advice and encouragement from parents and relatives are fine, but depending upon them is childish. Mature adults cherish their parents and spend time with them. Yet they do not let their parents take care of them. If you still live with your parents, be respectful of their provision, but do not let it spoil you. Also, realize that you may have to exert extra effort to separate from them. God intends for men and women to cease from depending upon their parents, develop their own relationships, and depend upon Jesus Christ (Ephesians 5:31-33).

Baggage Issue #9: Parent-Child Relationships

God never designed humans to be our primary source for love, purpose, or security. Christ wants to supply all of those needs for us. However, the flesh will tempt people to believe that romantic, human love is more fulfilling than God's unconditional love. When immature singles believe this lie, they might seek a dating relationship as their primary means of comfort, guidance, and support. They consciously or subconsciously take on the role of a helpless maiden in distress or a guy down on his luck. Their desire to be rescued fosters a parent-child dating relationship. In essence, the needy person uses someone to be his or her mature protector. These roles are fine for children, but for adults, this kind of relationship is dangerous.

A parent-child dating relationship locks adults into unhealthy roles. The strong person is conned into serving as a parent, and the needy person clings like a leech. The weak individual has little desire to grow up; he or she simply wants a free ride. However, the strong individual is also needy in a different way. He or she needs the weak person's dependence to feel significant.

Parent-child dating relationships occur when one person relies on the other to make decisions and provide self-control, protection, or integrity. The weak individual tries to substitute his or her poor character with someone else's. Avoid dating relationships with those who rely upon you to be their maturity. The attention and flattery from an immature person may feel good, but you cannot be his or her savior. Passionate dating relationships only happen between two mature adults.

Confronting Relational Baggage

People rarely volunteer information about their baggage, and some singles do not realize that they carry any. In either case, they may rationalize that no problem exists. Therefore, if you notice any odd behavior from the person you date, you must initiate the discussion tactfully. Baggage never resolves itself. The sooner you confront it, the easier it is to handle.

Get Baggage on the Table

Before you get to a serious level in a dating relationship, you need to discover whether you or your date carries any baggage. This means uncovering the truth about someone before discussing marriage. Be sure, however, that you have a reasonable amount of rapport before you begin this kind of dialogue. Baggage issues can be very touchy subjects for some people, so you must use tact and discretion. Be firm but not aggressive.

Baggage is easier to discuss when you can work the subject into normal conversation. You might start a discussion by saying, "Did you hear what happened to so-and-so? Has something like that ever happened in your life?" or "I enjoy our dating relationship, and I am interested in going deeper together. However, I am curious or concerned about your _____. Could we talk about it openly? I would like to know the truth." These are good ways to lovingly introduce a negative topic.

Should an outside source allege that your boyfriend or girl-friend has a checkered past, calmly bring it up for discussion with your date. Mention that you heard some interesting stories about him or her. Ask whether the stories are true. If your date answers yes, then ask whether he or she is still engaged in that activity. You might also say, "You seem distant or guarded whenever we talk about _____. Your past is important to me, and I would like to know more details." Remember to wait until you have been dating a while before confronting baggage. Diplomacy is very important. You can scare your date off or shut him or her down if you push too hard. Nevertheless, dealing with the tough issues before you give your heart away is imperative.

In addition, be honest if someone confronts you about your baggage. Do you regret something in your past? You don't have to pull out your skeletons on the first date, but you should share your baggage issues before your relationship gets serious. Likewise, don't feel like you have to share all of the sordid details. Just give the other person enough information to understand your past.

The point of dating is to love sacrificially, which involves swallowing your pride so that someone can know the truth about you. Sometimes, this means volunteering information about your past to give the other person an accurate picture of you.

When Ashley and I started dating, we had several long discussions about my previous marriage. I opened the door to honest conversation by telling Ashley that she could ask me anything. Also, I welcomed questions from her parents about my past to make sure they were comfortable with our new relationship. Lastly, we visited a Christian counselor who helped confirm that I had properly dealt with the pain of my first wife deserting me. Those steps assured Ashley that my heart had healed and that I was willing to make a lifetime commitment to her.

Baggage Claim

Suppose that harmful baggage surfaces in your dating relationship. How do you deal with it in a healthy way? First, resist the temptation to come to a quick, emotional decision. Don't criticize the person or automatically suppose he or she is evil or immature. A person who is willing to deal with baggage can offer the potential for a great relationship. You just might need to progress more slowly than you originally intended. Second, when someone shares his or her dark secrets with you, remember that you also have made mistakes. Jesus died for your date's sin just as He died for yours. Do not judge the person, but consider how his or her baggage might negatively affect your relationship.

If your boyfriend or girlfriend's baggage makes you feel uncomfortable, do not ignore your concern. The agitation in your heart may be the Holy Spirit advising you to date cautiously. Inform your date about your misgivings and expect the person to understand the harmful effects his or her baggage could have on the relationship. Give someone the chance to deal with the problem if he or she exhibits a sincere desire to change. Take your time, and make sure the person addresses the issues completely. However, if he or she shows no genuine interest in dealing with baggage, end the relationship for your and the other person's good.

Seek a Trained Christian Counselor

When you discover baggage about your date, resist the urge to try to fix it yourself or play the role of counselor. Your romantic emotions can cloud your reasoning and discernment.

Also, if you try to counsel your boyfriend or girlfriend, you risk developing a relationship based on pity. You might treat him or her as a sick puppy rather than as an adult who needs to grow up.

Relational baggage such as addiction, sexual abuse, or debt is too complex to remove with affection or words of encouragement. It requires help from a trained Christian counselor. Most people aren't aware of all the repercussions that their baggage can cause. More damage usually exists than what you see on the surface. For example, alcoholism is not simply a problem with drinking too much. Alcoholism can also include an overall lack of judgment, a willingness to hide the truth, and a lack of trust in God and other people. An alcoholic needs to correct all of these destructive issues to find freedom.

If you or your date struggle with any baggage issues, I encourage you to seek counseling. Furthermore, you might want to put your relationship on hold until the problem is fully healed. Getting assistance not only opens the road to recovery but also shows a desire to improve the relationship. Anyone who neglects counseling demonstrates a lack of care for the person he or she is dating.

Christian counselors facilitate healing by helping someone completely work through his or her incorrect beliefs and flesh patterns. They are trained to help people break free from baggage by applying the unconditional acceptance of Jesus directly to the problem. They listen objectively and ask the tough questions. They also provide a comfortable environment to thoroughly discuss concerns, fears, and consequences. Keep in mind, however, that counselors are human and imperfect. Listen to what they say but request Scripture and examples that support their advice.

If you have trouble locating a counselor in your area, visit the websites of Focus on the Family (www.fotf.org) or the American Association of Christian Counselors (www.aacc.net) for updated information. If you still have difficulty getting help, ask your friends or pastor whom they recommend. Be careful not to expose scandalous personal problems about you or your date by asking friends for advice. Simply ask for the name of someone who has experience handling the specific issue. Find a professional who specializes in treating the baggage that concerns you.

Be wary of asking secular counselors to assist with baggage issues. If they are atheists, they can only treat the symptoms instead of the root. Sometimes, secular counseling relies too much on self-analysis, medication, or self-improvement methods. However, these won't fix the problem because relational baggage usually correlates to a person's understanding of God. People ultimately find release from their struggles when they learn to apply Christ's love to their situation.

At some point, you might date someone who refuses to deal with his or her baggage. In that case, breaking up may be your best option. In the next chapter, we'll discuss how the pure passion of Christ can guide you through that difficult decision.

Personal Bible Study

1. What insight does 1 Timothy 6:6-11 offer about debt or the love of money?

2. Look up 1 Corinthians 6:9-11 and Ephesians 2:1-5. What good news in these verses can you apply to overcoming an addiction?

3. What solution to overcoming sexual baggage can you draw from Colossians 3:5-12?

4. Read Proverbs 13:20 and 1 Corinthians 15:33. Do you spend most of your time with people who have character? Ask God whether you should end any friendships with imprudent people who negatively influence you.

5. Examine the list of relational baggage mentioned in 2 Timothy 3:1-9. Observe if the person you date struggles with any of these problems. If so, what can you do to address the issue and protect yourself?

6. What assistance does God offer in John 14:16-17,26-27 that can help you discern harmful baggage in your relationships?

Group Discussion Questions

1. How does relational baggage originate within a person? Why are Christians not immune to carrying baggage?

2. Survey your group to find out what types of relational baggage they have encountered most frequently in dating. What problems did this baggage cause in those relationships? How would you advise friends to handle someone who carries that particular kind of baggage?

3. Discuss how the life of Christ living through a Christian offers freedom from addiction.

4. What are the dangers of dating again too quickly after a relationship ends (rebounding)?

5. Identify other types of relational baggage not covered in this chapter that you have personally encountered. What problems did they cause?

6. Discuss the benefits of meeting with a Christian counselor to deal with baggage issues. Can anyone in your group recommend a good Christian counselor to contact?

11

THE COMPASSION OF PASSION

:: :: ::

Breaking Up with Sensitivity

*M*y first serious girlfriend was named Diane. We were classmates in high school and developed a romantic relationship upon returning home from different colleges. After a year of dating, we shared such an intense chemistry that we nicknamed each other "soul mate" and began to consider marriage.

Therefore, I was stunned when Diane abruptly ended our relationship one evening. She handed me a list of reasons for breaking up and told me goodbye. Astonished, I couldn't accept her decision and lost control of myself. All I remember is a humiliating episode of crying, clamoring, and begging on my knees for a second chance. The awful event climaxed with her struggling to steady me as I threw up all over her parent's garage. It was the most embarrassing moment of my life.

In all fairness to Diane, she had good rationale for ending our relationship. We had expressed different plans about our future, but I was too focused on our romantic affection to consider our differences. She left to follow her dream of living overseas while I brooded for months over losing her.

I was already a Christian at that point but was unaware of Christ's passionate love for me. Diane was the center of my life, so losing her also meant losing my sense of significance. After we broke up, I felt a desperate need to find another woman who could replace Diane's love. This pressure dominated me as I renewed my dating life.

Meeting new women was scary because I depended upon their acceptance for my self-esteem. I faked calmness, but in reality I felt like an unsettled mess. My hunger for approval eventually led me to date a woman simply because she showed interest in me. It was a stupid relationship because we had little in common, but I couldn't turn down her attention. I pretended to be interested just to have a woman in my life. As you can guess, our relationship didn't amount to much. We soon parted, and the pain in my heart lingered.

My tumultuous finale with Diane illustrates the lasting consequences of a breakup. It is a crossroads type of experience because *the behavior that you exhibit during a breakup can affect the quality of your next relationship.* When Diane broke up with me, she handled the situation firmly but politely. It wasn't an easy decision for her. Yet her sensitivity reduced her chances of developing emotional baggage that could sabotage her future relationships. In my case, however, I separated from Diane in anger and desperation. My immature response began to degrade my self-esteem as well as my attitude toward women. All of that distress negatively affected my next relationship.

Dating is essentially an exploratory process, which means that no relationship is guaranteed to succeed. Human romance does not come with any assurances, so a painful breakup could likely happen to you in the future. Furthermore, the way you handle that situation can influence subsequent relationships. Don't worry though because the love of Christ can inspire you to end a relationship in a healthy way.

Let Jesus Handle a Breakup

In chapter 3, we discovered that God does not cause the difficulties of life, including the end of a dating relationship. However, God may encourage singles to stop dating for beneficial reasons, such as

1. getting out of a dead-end or abusive relationship
2. regaining objectivity about a boyfriend or girlfriend
3. focusing again on their spiritual marriage without distraction
4. pursuing another calling

Regardless of the reasons for a breakup, rude, desperate, or insensitive behavior only makes things more difficult for both of you. Jesus offers a better alternative—He wants to handle a breakup for you. He wants the best for both of you and knows how to manage a respectful separation through you.

When Christ walked the earth 2000 years ago, He understood the pain of a broken relationship. Indeed, He suffered the ultimate breakup on the cross when He endured the rejection of mankind (Luke 23:20-25). However, Jesus did not hurl insults or threats at those who crucified Him. Instead, He remained compassionate and asked God to forgive humanity (Luke 23:34). Because of His understanding of relationships, Christ wants to live His life through you when a breakup occurs. This applies whether you initiate or receive the farewell. He offers His dignity and compassion to replace the chaos of your emotions.

When you let Christ handle a breakup, you do not bypass the pain or displeasure of the situation. You still need to acknowledge your feelings, but Jesus wants to bolster you in those painful moments with His love. He wants you to accept the circumstance, move on with your life, and know that He will bring new people across your path.

To Jesus, a breakup is not about winning or losing. You are not the victor if you decide to break up first. Instead, He views a dating separation as an opportunity for His love to further impact your lives. Since the end of a relationship does not factor into your true identity, you do not need to attack or cling to your boyfriend or girlfriend. You are not a failure if someone breaks up with you. Neither are you superior if you decide to stop seeing someone.

This is your real identity: You are an unconditionally loved, accepted, and forgiven child of God. This truth is imperative to keep in mind when you experience all the emotions of a breakup. You may feel distressed and insecure, but Jesus loves you and promises that your future is in His care (1 Peter 5:7). I can attest that when you allow Christ to handle a breakup, you can look back on it with thanksgiving. In the next section, we will examine the benefit of His involvement when you choose to stop seeing someone. Then we will discuss the importance of His love, should someone break up with you.

The Benefits of a Clean Break

Michelle had high hopes for her relationship with Alan. But after four months, issues cropped up that made her wonder about their compatibility. Alan neglected to attend church with Michelle, and it bothered her to watch him treat spiritual issues flippantly. Their time together also revealed differences in their personalities, their preferences in friends, and their spending habits. Michelle liked Alan but struggled to see their relationship as a good fit. After pouring out her feelings to a wise friend and praying about the situation, she decided to call things off.

Michelle knew that the longer she waited, the harder it would be to break up, so she called Alan early the following evening. Her nerves were shaky as they engaged in small talk, but Michelle silently asked Jesus to live through her, and then she dropped the news. "Alan, I need to be honest with you," she said. "I have enjoyed our time together, but I do not think that we are on the same page spiritually. I think it is best that we end our relationship. Please don't hear me say that I think you are a bad guy. You have been nice to me, and I will respect you if our paths cross again."

Initially, Alan objected and urged her to give their relationship a second chance. Nevertheless, Michelle held her resolve. "Alan, I know you might be upset, but I believe that breaking up is the best thing for both of us. Please remember that God loves you more than any woman ever will. He has a great future planned for you. We will both be okay, and I ask you to accept my decision."

Breaking up with someone is rarely easy because mixed emotions of discontent and friendship tend to complicate the separation. To keep emotions from dominating the end of a relationship, I recommend making a clean break. *A clean break occurs when you break up respectfully, end the relationship, and completely stop seeing each other.* Both parties peacefully separate and return any personal belongings. Then, if they bump into each other in public, they are cordial to each other but avoid any discussion of getting back together. Should they again feel a mutual attraction, they wait several months before reuniting. Let's discuss the benefits to breaking up in this manner.

Benefit #1: You Value the Other Person

A breakup is a relational turning point, which means that you can choose to enhance or degrade your relational growth. A clean break gives you the opportunity for maturity. It not only suggests a complete separation but also treats the other person with respect. Your boyfriend or girlfriend has great value to Jesus Christ (He died on the cross for that person). Though the person may no longer be right for you to date, Jesus still has wonderful plans for him or her.

It is possible to communicate value to someone as you break up by showing courtesy and reminding the person of his or her worth to Christ. By doing so, you consider the needs of others as important as your own, and you foster the right attitude when your next relationship comes along.

When you end a relationship, you may feel tempted to gloat or to belittle the other person. However, rude behavior can numb your heart from caring about another person in the future. An air of superiority or a desire for control generally stays with you. Thus, you might start dating again with a self-centered attitude. Obviously, this decreases your ability to love someone in the future.

However, if you show respect when you break up, offering kindness, forgiveness, politeness, and firmness, you can more easily love the next person you date. You cannot experience a passionate dating relationship if you love sacrificially only on occasion. The maturity to love someone comes from allowing Christ to love through you, which occurs as you continually yield to Him by faith. Thus, loving a person during a breakup presents the opportunity to rely upon Jesus for His life.

Some singles, however, hesitate to break up with someone because they worry about hurting the other person's feelings. This may sound kind, but it is actually rude. If your boyfriend or girlfriend begins to disinterest you, he or she can usually tell it. People can sense when someone loses appreciation for them. Worse, you dishonor a person when you fake an interest but wish to be somewhere else. Instead, Jesus urges you to value a person by compassionately letting him or her go.

A clean break does not mean that you reject the person; it means that you reject the relationship. You might be justifiably upset by the way your boyfriend or girlfriend has treated you. Yet you still have no reason to devalue him or her. Trashing another person's self-esteem harms you as well; it degrades your maturity. On the other hand, a clean break emphasizes the person's value in God's eyes. I'm not suggesting that you give someone a syrupy farewell, but you can show respect. We will look at some practical examples later in this chapter.

Benefit #2: Less Overall Pain

Though a clean break may produce intense initial pain, it reduces the overall, long-term pain for both parties. It gives closure, which allows your heart to immediately begin the healing process. Otherwise, you can struggle endlessly with indecision or a false hope of getting back together. A clean break permits you to carry on with life.

If you break up with someone but continue to spend time together, your heart can remain confused and distracted by that person. You both stay in a relational rut with little freedom to get involved with new people or activities. It is a dead-end situation and actually prolongs your pain and prevents the healing process. Conversely, a clean break allows faster healing for both of you. The sooner you start to heal, which includes grieving the loss of the relationship, the sooner you can meet someone who is a better fit. A clean break removes distraction so you can be available for what God wants to do next in your social life.

Benefit #3: Avoids the "Let's Just Be Friends" Issue

Some singles, usually women, fret over breaking up because their relational side wants to remain friends. Unfortunately, once a romantic relationship has started, it's almost impossible to revert to a platonic friendship. God did not design romance to move backward.

A clean break does away with the friendship dilemma. Rather than say, "Let's just be friends," cleanly separate and end all communication for at least two or three months. (I suggest a longer separation if you were engaged in sensual activity.) This kind of split includes staying apart if you meet in public and ceasing all phone calls, e-mails, letters, or get-togethers.

A clean break does not prevent you from being friends with your ex-boyfriend or ex-girlfriend in the future. You split long enough, however, for your hearts to fully heal. Once both of you have recovered, you can reconsider being friends. How do you know when it is right to renew communication? When you no longer need a relationship in order to feel complete.

Telling someone that you no longer want to be friends is neither ungodly nor impolite. To grow relationally as an adult, you need friends who are mature and considerate. If your boyfriend or girlfriend cannot provide that kind of relationship, then you are smart to separate completely and make time for someone else.

Your heart cannot heal from a relationship when you stay close to your ex or leave the door open to getting back together. A clean break not only helps you move on but also gives you objectivity about the person. This unbiased attitude can be useful in assessing whether that person is right for you, should you renew a romance down the road.

When You Want to Call It Quits

As we discussed in chapter 4, God does not want you to date someone who is immature, unromantic, or selfish. Thus, you may want to break up if you do not feel comfortable or share a genuine attraction with someone. However, before you decide to call it quits, consider whether you have given your relationship a fair shot and prepare to be sensitive.

Did You Give Your Relationship a Chance?

Even the best dating relationships have their problems. If you cannot learn to forgive and compromise within dating, you will hinder your maturity for marriage. Give your date a fair chance to deal with negative issues, and don't pass immediate judgment. This doesn't imply that you should ignore immature behavior, character defects, or incompatible beliefs. But when something bothers you about your boyfriend or girlfriend, mention your concern and give your date the opportunity to respond— expecting him or her to take the issue seriously.

Sometimes God uses dating relationships to teach you how to be compassionate when someone is struggling. Therefore, be patient with your boyfriend or girlfriend's mistakes until you have a valid reason to break up. Disappointment and conflict are part of life. Consequently, it is unrealistic to expect that every moment of your relationship will be exhilarating.

Some singles are perfectionists and have a hard time accepting other people's faults. They date using a hypercritical standard and immediately reject anyone who fails to measure up. Their high expectations, however, reveal relational immaturity because no perfect people exist. Sin has marred everyone. Thus, their desire for a perfect boyfriend or girlfriend is a sign of selfishness. They want someone else to make them happy.

If you frequently dump your dates the moment they disappoint you, you may never learn how to stay committed in a marriage. Before you decide to break up, consider if you have given your relationship a fair chance. Try the following list of questions as a gauge:

1. Have you confronted your date about issues that bother you? If so, was he or she willing to change?
2. Do you judge your relationships based on how happy you feel?
3. Are you uncomfortable with the idea of committing yourself to one person?
4. Have you dated long enough to get a clear picture of the other person?
5. Do your friends or family like the person you are dating?

Let your answers from these questions help you determine whether you are quick to judge those you date. In addition, remember that it takes many months to develop compatibility, trust, and sacrifice with someone. Be patient. However, if you don't see any future together once you have given someone a fair shot, then breaking up is the wise thing to do.

Be Sensitive When You Break Up

If you are ready to end a relationship, be sensitive. Emotional comments can act as fuel on a fire. It takes only one sarcastic remark for a discussion to escalate into a bitter argument. Therefore, plan how you can minimize the emotion when you break up with someone. Choose a time and setting that allows you to easily say your final words and move on.

For instance, your date might overreact if you break up late at night, during a frustrating day, or at a familiar romantic spot. Think about how you can convey the news in the most comfortable way for both of you. Sometimes the best way to break up is over the phone. You can plan your words in advance and end the conversation quickly if the other person responds irrationally.

When you state why you want to end a relationship, keep your words to a minimum. The longer you talk, the more you risk your emotions intensifying. Also, I suggest discussing your reasons for breaking up in terms of "the fit." You can tell the other person, "This relationship isn't a good fit for me," or "I want the best for you, and we are not a good fit." These are true statements that don't attack the other person's self-worth.

Your boyfriend or girlfriend might demand an explanation for the breakup. He or she may even promise to change if you explain why you feel dissatisfied. Frankly, you are not obligated to explain your reasons. However, it is polite to give the other person some closure. If you feel comfortable clarifying your decision, be as brief and tactful as possible with any negative comments. Bear in mind the vulnerability that someone can feel during a breakup.

In only a few instances is it beneficial during a breakup to detail your complaints about someone (for example, when someone refuses to deal with his or her baggage, such as debt, addictions, codependency, or personality disorders). If you previously confronted the person about the problem, but he or she refused to deal with it, mention your frustration. The person needs to understand the impact of his or her immature behavior on other people. Review the following sample conversations for ideas on how to spell out your concerns:

> Jeremy, I've enjoyed our time together. Unfortunately, your debt of $30,000 worries me, and I do not feel confident in your ability to resolve the problem. I am ending

> our relationship, but I know that God loves and promises
> to take care of you.
>
> Beth, you are a nice person, and I'm glad that we have
> dated. However, I feel frustrated because you dominate
> our conversations. It is difficult for us to communicate
> when I can't participate in a discussion. Therefore, I think
> it is best if we discontinue our relationship.

Remember that when you break up, you want to end the relationship without diminishing the value of your date. This is possible when you have a firm but polite conversation. Attempt to express that your separation is no reason for the other person to feel inferior. Assure the person that Christ loves him or her completely and has good plans ahead (Romans 8:15-18). You might even compliment the person on his or her personality, appearance, character, family, or hobbies. However, be careful not to give false hope that you might get back together.

Do not be surprised if the person gets upset or protests emotionally. He or she may become defensive and blame all of the problems on you. If this happens, don't argue. A breakup is not about determining who is right or wrong because both people are usually at fault in some way. You simply want to end the relationship and move on in a respectful manner.

Be sure to be diplomatic because you will likely see the person again. If you antagonize or offend someone, you could come across as immature. Remember that your success in dating can be determined by your reputation. People talk, so you never want to burn a bridge with disrespectful behavior. Instead, extend compassion during a breakup, and you will exhibit a maturity that people will notice. For example, I have a good friend who peacefully separated with one girl and wound up marrying her sister a few years later. If he had been rude to the first sister, he might not have the wonderful wife he cherishes today.

Finally, once you have ended a dating relationship, keep private your dissatisfaction with the other person. Spreading news about your ex's problems is gossip and makes you look bad. Also, resist the temptation to report someone's problem as a prayer request. I've heard comments such as, "Please pray for Mike. I ended our relationship because of his pornography addiction." If you break up with someone who has a serious struggle, ask for his or her permission to tell someone about it or anonymously find professional assistance for the person.

When Rejection Strikes You

Remember the story of my painful breakup with Diane at the beginning of the chapter? I didn't mention the numerous ways I attempted to win her back. I wrote love letters and secretly placed them at her front door in the middle of the night. I cornered her at church and urged her to reconsider our romance. I even tried to get her friends to take my side and convince her to date me again. Nothing worked.

Unfortunately, this desperate, immature crusade did not stop with Diane. It festered within me as I met new single women. My inability to handle dating rejection increased my craving for the approval of a woman. I was compelled to find a new romance to erase the pain of losing Diane and prove that I was worthy of a girlfriend. This meant that I selfishly dated to find a woman to make me happy—loving her was secondary. That's not God's idea of dating with pure passion.

How did God finally transform me to love in a healthy way? He used my relationship with Diane and other painful rejections to expose my misplaced craving for a woman's acceptance. As I mentioned in chapter 1, I was essentially trying to live on "chocolate" love when I needed something more nutritious. My heart remained hungry until I discovered the reality of God's unconditional love for me. Then His acceptance filled my heart and gave me love to share.

In this sinful world, your heart will taste romantic rejection. The sudden loss of a dating relationship can be quite a blow. How can Christ's love sustain you during and after a breakup?

Breaking Up Is Not the End of the World

When a boyfriend or girlfriend breaks up with you, you initially might beg for the relationship to continue. I can assure you, however, that pleading only makes the person lose respect for you. If he or she has decided to leave, it's best to let go for two reasons.

First, when someone ends a serious dating relationship with you, the person is usually doing you a favor. By "favor," I mean that your date has released you to pursue a relationship that is a better fit. If someone is not motivated to be with you, then dating him or her is an unhealthy waste of time. Your emotions may feel otherwise, and that's understandable. But you cannot change someone's mind if he or she no longer wants to date you. It is best to let that person go and to view your new freedom as an opportunity to find a better relationship with someone who sincerely wants to be with you.

You may feel as if your old boyfriend or girlfriend was the right person for you. But how could that person be right if he or she has no interest in loving you? Breaking up removes you from a dead-end position so that you can share the passion of Christ with someone who wants to reciprocate.

Second, you damage your self-esteem when you clamor to another person for love. Remember that only Christ, not other people, can fulfill your heart with the unconditional love that it needs. By begging another person for love, you permit Satan to make you feel worthless. His goal is to convince you that you are ugly and unlovable. When a boyfriend or girlfriend rejects you, Satan tends to badger your mind with such thoughts as *Nobody will ever love me* or *Only losers sit at home by themselves on a weekend.*

If you believe his lies, the devil can trick you into feeling miserable or try to make you desperate for another relationship. He will claim that God's love is useless to a broken heart, and the only way to recover is to date again as soon as possible. Satan wants to lead you into an anxious search for another person's acceptance.

His goal is to keep your self-esteem dependent on the love of people rather than the love of Christ.

Another more subtle consequence of mishandling rejection is that you lose respect for the opposite sex. For instance, after a breakup, a woman may transfer her anger and disappointment onto her next boyfriend. If her pain festers for a long time, she may even develop hatred toward men in general. She might think, *Men are all the same* or *You can't trust any man*. Likewise, men upset over the loss of a girlfriend may spitefully characterize all women as only useful for sex. This attitude reveals a fear of the opposite sex that remains from a past relationship. Plenty of cruel men and women live in this world, but generalizing their behavior over the entire population is ridiculous. If you do so, your bad attitude can ruin your next relationship. That's why having the proper perspective during a breakup is important.

So how do you deal with the pain of a disheartening breakup? Grieve the loss of your relationship, but remember that a rejection does not define you. Satan will attempt to make you feel lonely, insecure, or uncertain. Meanwhile, Jesus will minister to you with thoughts about His support, acceptance, and care for you. His love is your heart's best protection from depression because Jesus is the only Person who will never forsake you. He loves you unconditionally, and your future in Him is bright. This is true whether you believe it or not, but your faith makes it real in your life.

Your perspective makes all the difference during a breakup. You can take the rejection personally and fall into despair, or you can realize that the breakup releases you from dating the wrong person. Regardless of how good you think a relationship is, you don't want to date someone if he or she isn't interested in you.

A breakup is not the end of your world. Sure, it hurts, but remember the positives. You are free from an unhealthy situation, and your heart is forever sealed in Christ's love. As you patiently walk in Him, He will bring new people into your life with whom you can share His passion.

Character and Comfort from the Holy Spirit

Suffering a breakup affects your character because pressure from the disappointment, pain, and rejection forces you to decide what you truly believe. You have two choices: You can believe that the life of Jesus Christ will support you through the pain and mature you for future relationships, or you can run from your pain through some form of self-medication (such as alcohol, pornography, another relationship, romance novels, or busyness). Numbing your heart with these things only prolongs your pain and prevents you from maturing.

Leaning upon Jesus during a rejection, however, helps build the character you need for good relationships in the future. Yet how can Christ give you character when your heart is broken? Where do you find the ability to love when you are hurt and want revenge? You cannot create character in your own strength. Instead, Jesus wants to give you His character through the Holy Spirit.

> And not only this, but we also exult in our tribulations, knowing that tribulation brings about perseverance; and perseverance, proven character; and proven character, hope; and hope does not disappoint, because *the love of God has been poured out within our hearts through the Holy Spirit who was given to us* (Romans 5:3-5).

These verses explain that God does not expect you to muster up holy behavior during emotional turmoil. He knows that you may not feel loving when someone breaks up with you. Instead, He wants you to trust in Christ for His strength to bear the pain for you. Jesus has all of the hope, forgiveness, and strength you need to weather the storm. Allow Him to live it through you.

> But if the Spirit of Him who raised Jesus from the dead dwells in you, He who raised Christ Jesus from the dead will also *give life to your mortal bodies through His Spirit who dwells in you* (Romans 8:11).

When you became spiritually married to Jesus, God put Christ's life within you in the form of the Holy Spirit. He is your constant Helper, especially in times of sorrow, loss, and temptation. He offers peace and assurance that His love can sustain you through the hard times. However, the Holy Spirit cannot help you until you surrender your will to Him and stop looking for a quick fix. Christ knows what is best for you, and He might ask you to take a break from dating. If so, He will not force His will upon you but wait for you to lay down your agenda.

God can work a painful rejection for your good when it causes you to depend completely on the love of Jesus. Remember that God does not create trials or breakups. You live in a sinful world, and tribulation is the by-product. However, these difficulties can enhance your character and mature you.

> Dear brothers and sisters, whenever trouble comes your way, let it be an opportunity for joy. For when your faith is tested, your endurance has a chance to grow. So let it grow, for when your endurance is fully developed, you will be strong in character and ready for anything. If you need wisdom—if you want to know what God wants you to do—ask him, and He will gladly tell you. He will not resent your asking (James 1:2-5 NLT).

By depending upon God's wisdom, you can endure a rejection with His optimistic perspective on your worth, future, and disposition toward others. He promises to restore your broken heart to enjoy new relationships at the right time. You no longer need dating to make you feel complete. You are already a complete man or woman, able to touch others with the same comfort that Christ extends.

> Blessed be the God and Father of our Lord Jesus Christ, the Father of mercies and God of all comfort, who comforts us in all our affliction so that we will be able to comfort those who are in any affliction with the comfort

with which we ourselves are comforted by God (2 Corinthians 1:3-4).

When you allow God to comfort you during a breakup, you can one day share with someone else the hope and encouragement that He gave you. Your testimony can help restore a hurting heart to love and maturity. By guiding someone to the comfort of God, you help spread the power of His passion from person to person.

Break Up in the Love of Christ

After my painful breakup with Diane, the desperate feeling in my heart carried over into successive dating relationships. I experienced one frustrating romance after another. My outlook didn't change until years later when the love of Christ began to saturate my self-esteem. I was dating a girl named Rachel, but our relationship died after four months. Faced with the inevitable, we broke up on the phone one morning. However, I did not beg for another chance or attack her with insults. Instead, I sensed Christ asking me to let Him live His love through me. The result was a clean, gracious separation. Rachel and I calmly discussed our decision to split and then respectfully encouraged one another as we said goodbye. I still felt the disappointment, but it wasn't a crushing blow.

Consequently, I didn't walk away with emotional baggage that could ruin my next relationship. A year later, I started dating Ashley. As I look back, I credit Jesus for managing my breakup with Rachel and preparing me for my healthy relationship with Ashley. His desire within me to respect a woman, rather than use her, enabled me to date from a healthy perspective.

Ending a relationship is never easy, regardless of who initiates the breakup. Yet in the midst of the pain, confusion, and emotions, you have the opportunity to let Christ build your relational maturity. To Him, a breakup can be a wonderful turning point in your life. You may lose the passion of a romantic relationship, but you will never lose the passion that Jesus has for you.

On the other hand, maybe you are dating someone and a breakup is the last thing on your mind. You wonder instead whether you should get married. The next chapter offers some questions to help you clarify that decision.

Personal Bible Study

1. Chapter 11 states, "The behavior that you exhibit during a breakup can carry over to affect the quality of your next relationship." How does Galatians 6:7-10 apply to that statement?

2. In Luke 10:10-11, Christ directed the disciples to leave a town that wasn't interested in a relationship with them. Would you agree that continuing to date someone who is not interested in loving you is detrimental? Why?

3. What hope and encouragement can you draw from Romans 8:15-18 when you face a breakup?

4. Name four helpful points in Ephesians 4:25-27,29 that would apply to a breakup conversation.

5. Read Galatians 5:13-15. What insight do these verses give that can apply to your attitude when breaking up with someone?

6. Consider the statements in Ephesians 2:19 regarding a Christian's identity. In light of this verse, how should you treat another Christian whom you date?

Group Discussion Questions

1. Discuss the benefits of a clean breakup as explained in chapter 11.

2. How can you love someone as you break up with him or her? Suggest various approaches to politely ending a dating relationship.

3. Consider how a hostile breakup could scar your ability to lovingly date someone in the future.

4. What are the negative consequences of listing someone's problems to him or her when you break up?

5. Is a breakup really the end of the world? What hope does God give Christians about their relational future?

6. Why is the life of Jesus Christ within you the best source of comfort when you lose a dating relationship?

12

EMBRACE
YOUR PASSION

:: :: ::

Questions to Consider Before You Get Engaged

$\mathcal{T}$he day I married Ashley, I must have been asked more than 50 times whether I was nervous. The barrage of questions surprised me because I had no reservations about giving her my heart. In my mind, I would have been a fool not to marry Ashley. Yet so many people questioned my composure that I began to worry whether something was wrong with me. I suddenly became anxious about not feeling nervous. Fortunately, as I dressed in my tuxedo, God reminded me that I had every good reason to marry Ashley and that He would uphold our marriage. I entered the church that evening with God's peace inspiring my steps.

If you are dating someone seriously, how peaceful do you feel when you think about marrying that person? Committing your heart to someone is a huge decision. If you choose poorly, you could suffer years of heartache or wind up abused or divorced. However, if you select a marriage partner wisely, you could enjoy a lifetime together of intimate love and passion.

Sadly, some couples rush toward marriage as soon as they taste the initial burst of romance. They may have only dated for a few months, but their blissful feelings convince them that they are destined for each other. By contrast, other couples date for years but never find the courage to make a commitment. They so dread marrying the wrong person that they do not marry at all. In the midst of these extremes, how can a single adult sensibly decide whom to marry?

The good news is that as a Christian, you are not alone in your decision-making process. You have Jesus Christ dwelling within you. He offers His divine wisdom in every situation so that you don't have to rely upon your emotions or finite wisdom.

> And God has actually given us his Spirit...so we can know the wonderful things God has freely given us.... But people who aren't Christians can't understand these truths from God's Spirit.... How could they? For, "Who can know what the Lord is thinking? Who can give him counsel?" But we can understand these things, for we have the mind of Christ (1 Corinthians 2:12,14,16 NLT).

God wants the best for you. He gave you the mind of Christ so you can perceive life from His perspective. Jesus can work through your heart and mind to direct you toward a good relationship and dissuade you from a bad one. However, you can only discern His counsel when you are willing to listen and yield to Him.

To Jesus, romantic passion is the wrong foundation for a marriage. He wants you to give your heart to someone on the basis of character and passionate sacrificial love. To help you assess if your relationship contains these elements, consider the following eight questions before you get engaged.

1. Are You Both Married to Jesus Christ?

This question pertains to the most important aspect of your relationship—the spiritual. If you or your date does not know Jesus as the primary Source of love, then you will try to manipulate love from one another. Remember from chapter 1 that depending upon performance-based human love is like eating chocolate—it may taste good, but it cannot satisfy you. Your heart needs more than romantic affection to survive; it needs unconditional love, which can only be found in Jesus Christ. Thus, it is best to marry someone who understands that he or she is married to Jesus and realizes the importance of depending upon Him for fulfillment.

You will struggle to find this kind of person, however, if you believe that you can enjoy true intimacy with a non-Christian. Many Christian singles make this mistake in dating and shortchange themselves. Let me explain why.

As Christians, Ashley and I are united in Jesus Christ. This means that the same Jesus who lives within me also lives within Ashley. Therefore, He can help us love one another more deeply. Jesus can love Ashley by desiring to do so through me, sometimes without her having to say anything.

For example, I have never enjoyed washing dishes, and Ashley dislikes doing laundry. Therefore, we agreed that I would wash and fold our laundry and she would wash the dishes. Yet many times in our marriage I have felt the distinct urge to wash the dishes for her. Ashley didn't ask me to do it. I just felt a desire to help her. Trust me, I know this desire didn't come from me because I hate scrubbing dirty plates. Jesus created an impulse within my heart to love Ashley in this way.

On other occasions, Christ has prompted me to spontaneously clean Ashley's car, compliment her, or stop what I was doing and hold her after she had had a bad day. When I have acted upon those urges, Ashley has often exclaimed, "How did you know what I needed? I never hinted or asked you to do those things." I knew what Ashley needed because Christ motivated me.

I don't have to struggle on my own to be a good husband to Ashley. I can rest and allow Jesus to love her through me. Since He lives within both of us, He knows when she is tired or frustrated and can prompt me to encourage her. Likewise, He can inspire Ashley to support me when I need encouragement. This kind of supernatural love creates a bond stronger than that of any non-Christian married couple.

Let me clarify that our marriage bond in Christ does not give Ashley and me some sort of spiritual voodoo. We cannot read each other's thoughts. Yet as we respond to the desires that Jesus puts within our hearts, He leads us to love one another in the best manner. This creates real intimacy. Joined together in Christ, Ashley and I share the same wish to glorify God, the same joys and sorrows, and the same Source of love—we are one (Ephesians 5:31-32).

I never experienced this kind of intimacy with my first wife. She expressed an interest in God while we dated but denied any faith in Him when she later deserted our marriage. Her "Christian" talk had merely been a ploy to gain my acceptance. As the early struggles of marriage hit us, our opposing spiritual beliefs became apparent. We hardly felt like partners. I often felt alone in the same room with her. We were not one.

You risk this type of division when you consider dating or marrying a non-Christian. If you join yourself to an unbeliever, you will be incapable of sharing real intimacy. Are you free to date a non-Christian? Yes, but the Bible states that it is not profitable (1 Corinthians 10:23). God views believers and unbelievers as opposites who have no potential for a deep union (2 Corinthians 6:14; 1 Corinthians 7:39).

Can a Christian get along with an unbeliever and have fun dating him or her? Sure. In fact, some non-Christians exhibit just as much honesty and sensitivity as some Christians do. However, if you marry an unbeliever, he or she will generally have a larger influence on the direction of your relationship.

I compare dating a non-Christian to mountain climbing and rappelling. Imagine that a Christian woman stands at the top of a mountain, and an unbelieving man stands at the bottom. If the unbelieving man wants to join her, he must decide on his own to make the journey up. The woman cannot pull the man up with her own strength or force him to climb. Should the man not want to climb the mountain, the woman will remain at the top by herself. Likewise, if the woman wants to be with the man, she will feel tempted to rappel down to his level. Otherwise, they could try to meet halfway, but then they would hang uncomfortably off the side of the mountain.

Using romance to coax a non-Christian to climb up to your spiritual level is unhealthy. Some call it "missionary dating," which is the process of trying to convert an unbeliever while dating him or her. Though evangelistic affection may sound noble, the idea is flawed in several ways.

1. A Christian cannot overpower a non-Christian's free will and force him or her to accept Christ.

2. An unbeliever might fake a conversion simply to gain your acceptance.

3. New Christians do not automatically have character or spiritual maturity.

4. A non-Christian cannot meet your need for love or security.

If you try to convert someone to Christ just so you can date and marry him or her, you cloud that person's spiritual decision with human romance. In addition, if someone professes faith in Christ solely so that he or she can date you, the person probably is not a Christian. A person becomes a Christian when he or she genuinely asks forgiveness for sin and accepts Christ as Lord of his or her life. Even if you lead someone to accept Christ, he or she may need years to develop the maturity necessary for sacrificial love in marriage.

Furthermore, if you date an unbeliever (or even an immature Christian), you will usually assume the role of spiritual parent. You become that person's connection to God, and he or she can improperly cling to you for spiritual direction and maturity. Therefore, your dating relationship becomes an unhealthy parent-child situation. Since you can't improve another person's character, the two of you will remain on unequal levels. For Christians and non-Christians, reliance on each other prevents you from learning to rely on Christ.

Spiritually disinterested singles can seem fun to date. Yet if you marry someone who doesn't love Jesus, you will limit your opportunity to share oneness. Instead, seek to date and marry a mature Christian single who embraces his or her spiritual marriage to Jesus. Then you will have a partner who can participate in divine intimacy with you.

2. Can You Resolve Conflict Together?

Some couples pleasantly coast through dating, get married, and then receive a shock when their first round of conflict hits. They are unaware that two imperfect people experience friction no matter how much they love each other. Conflict is an unavoidable part of life, and it can destroy a couple who hasn't learned how to properly resolve it.

In chapter 6, we discussed that sin indwells your body and tries to influence you in ways contrary to the desires that Christ puts within you. You might feel tempted to be insensitive, greedy, self-indulgent, manipulative, or hostile. When you succumb to these temptations in a relationship, a simple disagreement can escalate into an all-out war.

Recognize that these selfish urges originate from the sin within you, not from you. Therefore, part of resolving conflict is remembering that as Christians, you and your date are not evil. By separating sin from the person, you can more easily resolve disagreements.

For example, one night at a restaurant, Todd sarcastically criticized his girlfriend, Jan, for the way she was dressed. His words hurt Jan's feelings, but instead of firing back, Jan replied, "Todd, I know you don't like my outfit, but what you said was rude. Whatever has gotten under your skin is ruining our evening together. We can talk about my clothes, but there is no need to criticize me."

In this situation, Todd did not come up with the idea to mock the way Jan dressed. Indwelling sin initiated the urge to be rude, and he selfishly chose to respond to the temptation. Fortunately, Jan saw the problem for what it was—sin instigating criticism within Todd. Jan's awareness of the truth allowed her to help Todd discern the lie rather than respond to him spitefully. She wisely nipped the problem in the bud, preventing the situation from escalating.

Knowing that sin seeks to cause strife does not mean that you can avoid conflict. When you distinguish indwelling sin from the person, however, you can more positively reconcile arguments because you focus on identifying sin's lies rather than attacking one another.

A second important aspect of resolving conflict is allowing Jesus Christ to live His love through you. Allowing Him to meet your need for security and significance diminishes your motivation to attack or manipulate someone else. You still continue to voice your opinions and wishes, but Christ within you works to reach a solution that most benefits your relationship. This means you learn to give and take. Should you need to give, Christ will prompt you to be humble. Likewise, if it is your turn to receive, Jesus will lead you to accept in gratitude.

Only through your faith can Christ help you resolve your issues. As a couple, you both have to yield to His desires. So it is important that you deal with conflict several times before considering engagement. Determine whether both of you have shown a desire to compromise in past arguments. If not, does one of you try to bully the other with angry outbursts? If you've had trouble handling disagreements, consider dating longer to learn how to disagree cooperatively. If nothing improves, you may need to end your relationship.

Civilized arguments can benefit a relationship by exposing neglect, unrealistic expectations, or different points of view. Sometimes, neither person is wrong. Each one is simply approaching the same topic from unique perspectives. Therefore, do not try to avoid conflict but seek to resolve it in a loving, mature manner. If you cannot freely voice your opinions, you will live in miserable bondage to another person. Both parties should have the freedom to express their ideas and desires.

A relationship devoid of conflict may signal that one of you is either too passive or too afraid to be genuine. These attitudes are not conducive to an intimate marriage, and you should not continue dating if you cannot be authentic with each other. Healthy relationships foster an environment in which you have the freedom to disagree. Thus, before you get engaged, make sure you both feel free to be yourselves and know how to lovingly resolve conflict.

3. Have You Both Dealt with Your Baggage?

We saw in chapter 10 how relational baggage can develop when someone pursues fulfillment through a person, possession, or substance rather than the love of Christ. Baggage can surface in a variety of forms, such as addictions, eating disorders, abortion, debt, or divorce. Unfortunately, almost everyone carries some type of baggage, so do not assume that your boyfriend or girlfriend is immune. Before you give someone your heart, determine if he or she is wrestling with any baggage issues.

Also, understand that the consequences of certain baggage may never disappear completely. An addiction can keep someone in poor health. A divorced single may regularly have child custody problems. If you want to marry someone who happens to have these kinds of issues, you might face some very tough circumstances when the person's past resurfaces. If you are not prepared to deal realistically with them, the repercussions could easily dominate your relationship. Discuss your concerns with a Christian counselor if you feel unsure about how someone's past might affect you.

Please do not downplay relational baggage—it has the power to destroy your relationship. Sometimes, these complex, negative issues require years to resolve. Do not expect that marriage will make them disappear. You will generally have to wait until a person overrides his or her baggage with the truth of God's love before real healing takes place. Therefore, if your date carries emotional baggage, please vigilantly deal with it before you get engaged. Marrying someone who is free of baggage is worth the extra months or years of waiting.

4. Do You Have the Support of Friends and Family?

After I dated Ashley for nine months, many of my close friends and relatives began to urge me to pop the question. When I asked why, they remarked that "We think Ashley is a great girl," and "We think you guys are a good fit for each other." I took comfort in these comments. They were sincere because Ashley and I had spent a lot of time around our friends and family. Their opinion meant something because they had been a part of our relationship. Since I knew they wanted the best for us, their excitement reinforced my desire to marry Ashley.

In the same way, I encourage you to seek the support of your friends and family. Since these people generally know you well, they can offer helpful insight on whether you and your date are a good match. In addition, they are not as emotionally blinded as you are and may identify problem areas that you have overlooked.

Should someone raise a concern about your relationship, focus on the facts and do not hide the truth. Be willing to admit that you might have neglected a problem. Parents and friends are not always right, but you should consider their legitimate opinions. They may have years of marriage experience to back up their concerns, and ignoring them would be foolish. Listen with an open mind to what they say about your relationship. Remember, however, that the final decision rests solely in your hands. Parents and friends can state their feelings, but don't allow them to decide for you. Instead, let loved ones be resources to aid in your decision-making process.

When you make one of the biggest decisions of your life, having the support of your family and friends is a wonderful blessing. It not only gives you a sense of peace but also assurance that they will be there for you if times get hard. No married couple is an island. You will need the encouragement of others—especially if you have children. You endanger your dating relationship if you hide it from people. Instead, ask yourself if those near to you are excited about your relationship moving forward, and examine why or why not.

I remember facing the crowd when the pastor announced Ashley and me as "Mr. and Mrs. Robert Eagar." I turned and saw 225 smiling faces that seemed to say, "We are happy for you, and we will support your marriage in the future." This was a wonderful confirmation that I had made a wise decision. To this day, our friends and family are still excited about and supportive of our marriage. They go out of their way to encourage us and invite us to be a part of their lives. If we need help in any way, they will be there for us. Don't underestimate the benefit that those close to you can have on your relationship.

5. Have You Sought Pre-engagement Counseling Together?

We discussed the benefits of pre-engagement counseling in chapter 9. At the risk of being redundant, though, I want to suggest it once more because it is so helpful when you are interested in marrying someone. It is impossible to uncover by yourself every potential problem area of your relationship. Even wise friends and family can overlook negative warning signs. Therefore, seek a trained Christian counselor to discuss the details of your relationship before you get engaged. I promise it is well worth it even if you have to go out of your way to find it.

Ashley and I participated in eight weekly sessions of pre-engagement counseling together. The format was casual, which allowed us to openly share our fears and hopes. The counselor was perceptive and showed us areas that could cause problems for us in the future. For instance, we discovered that we deal with our free time quite differently. Ashley prefers to make a list of tasks and work on projects, while I prefer to lounge around, read, and talk. Initially, this was a source of frustration because we didn't appreciate what the other person wanted to do. Neither of us was right or wrong; we were just different. Fortunately, the counselor revealed this issue to help us become more sensitive to each other. Rather than fight about our free time, we learned to value what the other person prefers. This is just one example of how pre-engagement counseling improved the harmony of our relationship.

The decision to marry someone is so significant; please do not bypass the wisdom of outside counsel before engagement. If you can meet with someone trained to deal with relational problems, you can save yourself a lot of heartache. Furthermore, a good counselor can help save you from marrying the wrong person.

6. Do You Bring Out the Best in Each Other?

Jane had dated Ted for ten months when he brought up their first discussion about marriage. Jane liked Ted but felt unsettled about their future. A friend had recently remarked how Jane didn't seem to be herself since she started seeing Ted. This comment grabbed her attention.

Jane began to reflect over her relationship and noticed that Ted rarely seemed enthusiastic about her interests. Whenever she asked him to stop by her art class or volunteer together at church, he would made excuses. Jane began to sense that her life revolved around Ted's fishing, work, and softball schedules. He wasn't possessive; he just didn't show support for the things she enjoyed. A relationship with Ted meant that her individuality and interests took a back seat to his. The more Jane pondered, the less she felt comfortable about moving forward.

When you consider marriage with someone, ask yourself, *Does this person bring out the best in me?* This question may sound trivial, but its answer will reveal much about the future quality of your relationship. As we have seen throughout this book, God's purpose for dating and marriage is that two people share sacrificial love. For that reason, you want to find someone who is passionate about investing in your life and vice versa.

In healthy relationships, people help each other to flourish. I call this "relational cheerleading." I don't mean positive pep talks. Rather, relational cheerleading is creating an encouraging environment in which another person can safely try new experiences and grow as an individual. This type of supportive atmosphere fosters intimacy. You go beyond telling someone, "You can do it" and involve yourself in his or her accomplishments.

> And let us consider how to stimulate one another to love and good deeds (Hebrews 10:24).

Before I married Ashley, I never realized how wonderful it was to be with someone who brings out the best in me. It is an amazing blessing to live with a partner who says, "I believe in you," and "I am so proud of you." Furthermore, she gets involved and helps me press on when I feel depressed, scared, or insensitive. Her belief in me goes beyond mere words.

Let me give you a firsthand illustration. Writing this book had been a dream of mine for years. Nevertheless, I almost gave up five times while trying to finish the manuscript. The project kept getting bigger than I expected, so I frequently felt overwhelmed. Ashley's excitement to see me accomplish my goal made a huge difference. She not only encouraged me when I was frustrated but also got involved by critiquing what I wrote each week. She sacrificed her time, interests, and desires to invest in the realization of my dream. She helped bring out the best in me.

In the same way, I encourage you to honestly assess what kind of influence your boyfriend or girlfriend has upon your life. Does he or she truly care about your growth and maturity? Does he or she encourage you to meet new people, try new hobbies, and maintain your faith in God? Does he or she have a history of sacrificing time, money, or attention to support you physically and spiritually? Or does he or she simply use you for his or her happiness?

Many singles have been demoralized by dating an immature person. Dating someone who is selfish shuts down a person's desire to grow spiritually, expand his or her interests, or get involved with others. Instead, Christ wants singles to spur each other on to grow in love and maturity.

You can start this process by asking your boyfriend or girlfriend about his or her dreams and goals. What has he or she always wanted to do? In what area could he or she use your support? Determine how you might reasonably help your date achieve his or her desire. Then date each other long enough so that an extended pattern of supportive behavior can emerge. Remember that dating is a prelude to marriage, and marriage is a commitment to an imperfect person for his or her highest good. Marrying someone who is committed to helping you flourish is a delight. On the other hand, living alone is better than marrying someone who does not deeply care about you.

7. Is Leadership Properly Established in Your Relationship?

When you are dating, you always have the option to leave if someone acts unreasonably. In marriage, though, you make a lifelong commitment. Therefore, selecting wisely is imperative, especially when it comes to the issue of leadership. The leader generally determines the maturity level of a relationship, and the best way to discern how someone handles leadership is to observe him or her in dating. The individual who leads during dating usually will lead in marriage. Unfortunately, many singles wrestle with relational leadership for two reasons: Either they misunderstand how someone becomes a leader or they misinterpret the leader's true purpose.

Our culture suggests that anyone who wants to lead must exhibit superior performance to earn the title. If a leader makes too many bad decisions, he or she can be fired and replaced. This definition, however, is not how God determines the leader of a marriage relationship.

> But I want you to understand that Christ is the head of every man, and the man is the head of a woman, and God is the head of Christ.... For man does not originate from woman, but woman from man; for indeed man was not created for the woman's sake, but woman for the man's sake. However, in the Lord, neither is woman independent of man, nor is man independent of woman. For as the woman originates from the man, so also the man has his birth through the woman; and all things originate from God (1 Corinthians 11:3,8-12).

> For the husband is the head of the wife, as Christ also is the head of the church, He Himself being the Savior of the body. But as the church is subject to Christ, so also the wives ought to be to their husbands in everything. Husbands, love your wives, just as Christ also loved the church and gave Himself up for her (Ephesians 5:23-25).

These verses clearly explain how God established the leadership structure for husbands and wives in marriage. His hierarchy reaches beyond the roles of men and women. Consider the following points:

1. God is the Head of Christ.
2. Jesus is the Head of every man and woman.
3. A husband is the head of his wife.
4. A woman is subject to her husband.
5. A husband is to love his wife sacrificially, just as Christ loves the church.
6. Men and women are not independent of each other.

Notice how people receive their roles through God's choice, not through their performance. Jesus and husbands are assigned the positions of leadership. In God's eyes, their actions have no bearing upon their qualifications as leaders. He assigned Christ and men as the leaders, and they choose whether to assume that responsibility properly. Obviously, Jesus always obeys His Father and respects His leadership (John 5:30).

A husband faces the choice whether to follow Christ's leadership. When a husband tries to lead his wife independently of Christ's leadership, he sins. Likewise, God calls a wife to follow her husband's leadership, and she sins if she chooses to act independently of Christ and her husband.

God made leadership a simple arrangement. Men and women complicate the issue when they refuse to submit to Jesus Christ. For instance, a wife sins if she disregards her husband's leadership because he doesn't make her happy enough. A husband also sins when he ignores Christ's leadership because Jesus won't provide him with easy circumstances.

By contrast, when men understand the sacrifice Jesus made for them, they are more inclined to respect and follow Him. In turn, Christ can then live His sacrificial love through a husband to his wife. As the wife realizes that both Jesus and her earthly husband desire to give themselves up for her, she more naturally accepts their leadership. This may sound like a performance-based setup, but it's not. God says that we are called to subject ourselves to our respective heads regardless of their performance.

How do you know whether the person you date accepts God's leadership structure? Observe his or her willingness to lead or submit. Ladies, does your boyfriend follow Jesus and love you sacrificially? Guys, does your girlfriend follow Jesus and respect your decisions? If not, you may be dating an immature person. When someone is unwilling to try out his or her relational role in dating, he or she will unlikely embrace it in marriage. Passive or dominating behavior boils down to a lack of faith in the authority of Christ.

Besides equating leadership with performance, some singles do not understand what leadership truly involves. God's definition of a leader is not simply "decision maker." A real leader sacrifices his desires for the benefit of his wife. God says that the man's job is to love his wife just as Christ loved the church. How did Christ express love for the church? He sacrificed His life so that He could have intimacy with us.

In the same manner, God urges men to love their wives sacrificially. Her needs and concerns are supposed to become his focus. In addition, his role includes maintaining an environment of intimacy. This means accepting her, forgiving her, protecting her, and considering her interests as more important than his. When a husband loves his wife sacrificially, he creates a physical illustration of Christ's love for believers. Therefore, ladies, observe whether the man you date behaves in this way. Does he know what is important to you? Does he sacrifice his interests for yours? Is he willing to disagree with you when he believes it is for your benefit?

Keep in mind that you cannot lead or submit to someone by relying on your brainpower or self-control. Instead, Jesus wants you to carry out your assigned roles *by allowing Him to live His life through you.* In a human relationship, Christ can simultaneously express submission through a woman and leadership through a man. He demonstrated both of these roles 2000 years ago on earth as He submitted to His heavenly Father while loving mankind sacrificially. Jesus wants to do the same through you today. Therefore, as you date someone, consider whether you have submitted your relationship to His leadership.

8. Are You Truly Passionate About Each Other?

Now that you have almost finished reading this book, you realize that my definition of the word *passion* does not refer to excitement or sexual lust. Instead, Jesus best defined *passion* when He innocently died on a cross out of love for you. He was so excited to be married to you that He sacrificed Himself even though you aren't perfect. This brings us to the final question to consider before you get engaged to someone: Are you passionate enough to sacrifice yourselves for each other, knowing full well that both of you are imperfect? In other words, are you so spiritually, sexually, mentally, and emotionally attracted to each other that you also accept one another's ugly, weak, and selfish faults?

Guys, do you feel just as interested in your girlfriend when she removes her makeup? Are you willing to drop your pride and cherish her during her mood swings? Are you willing to go out of your way to make sure she feels appreciated? Do you love her enough to seek her best interests even if that means denying your wishes or telling her no?

Ladies, are you more concerned with delighting your boyfriend than making yourself happy? Are you willing to love him even if he neglects or offends you? Do you adore him so much that you are prepared to follow him wherever God leads?

Marriage involves loving someone even if he or she disappoints, irritates, or ignores you. If you do not think that your boyfriend or girlfriend has any flaws, I encourage you to date longer. No one is perfect, and you set yourself up for relational failure if you expect marriage to be smooth and easy. Jesus knew the awful reality of your sin, but He felt such passion that He still chose to marry you. You make this kind of commitment when you choose to marry someone.

God wants Christ's pure passion to sustain your relationship. On some days the romance will fade, and you will feel bored with each other. How will you stay committed? Your spiritual marriage to Christ will supply the strength you need when times are hard. Jesus knows that you cannot maintain intimacy with someone because your ability to love is limited. Yet His devotion to the person you marry never wanes, so He can uphold your relationship by living His passion through you.

As a Christian, you no longer have to struggle to love. You possess the love of Christ within you, and the purpose of dating and marriage is to bond with someone in His divine passion.

Examine Your Passion

After examining your dating relationship in light of these questions, you may not feel a peace about committing to your boyfriend or girlfriend. That's okay. Dating benefits you because you can learn who someone is before you pledge your heart. Your discomfort may be the Lord urging you to date longer or to separate. If you break up, be glad that you avoided an unwise marriage decision. On the other hand, if you answered yes to the eight questions in this chapter, Jesus may be leading you toward marriage.

As husband and wife, Ashley and I are still amazed by how our hearts continue to unite in deeper ways. Our marriage has surpassed my wildest dreams of what romance, friendship, and love could ever be. We owe the pleasure to Christ, who pursued us with such love that we wanted to share it with someone else. Likewise, if Jesus is inspiring you to give yourself to someone special, then take the opportunity to pour His love into that person and relish the passionate relationship that He has waiting for you to explore together.

Personal Bible Study

1. Read 1 Timothy 4:3-5. God established marriage as a good gift for us to receive with gratitude. Do you desire to get married within these parameters, or do you seek marriage to meet your needs?

2. Read 2 Corinthians 6:14 and 1 Corinthians 7:39. Why do you think the apostle Paul urges Christians to marry other Christians only?

3. Examine Jesus' statement in John 5:30. In light of Jesus' example, how should men and women view the leadership and submission roles in marriage (and dating)?

4. Read Ephesians 5:21-33. In what way do these verses urge husbands and wives to love each other? If you are dating someone, are you both aware and accepting of these roles?

5. Turn to Hebrews 10:24 and Romans 15:2. What attitude in these verses can help you develop a mature, godly dating relationship?

6. According to Hosea 2:19-20, what six qualities describe how the Lord betroths Himself to you? If you are considering engagement, does your relationship exhibit these six qualities?

Group Discussion Questions

1. Discuss the parallels between earthly marriage and your spiritual marriage to Jesus Christ.

2. Why is resolving conflict in a loving manner beneficial to a dating relationship?

3. Should close friends and family be included in your decision to marry your boyfriend or girlfriend? Why or why not?

4. Talk about why you should date someone who brings out the best in you.

5. List three examples of how a husband could sacrifice himself to benefit his wife.

6. Define *pure passion* and discuss why it is necessary for a godly dating relationship.

13

PASSION
AWAITS YOU

‡ ‡ ‡

Conclusion

I have a close friend who works for a popular restaurant company. Because of his management position, he can invite guests to accompany him for dinner at no charge. Ashley and I have been fortunate to join him on several occasions, and we always enjoy a wonderful feast. We arrive hungry so that we have plenty of room to stuff ourselves with hearty cuisine.

Since we are allowed to order anything, we don't hold back. I usually start with a big salad loaded with fresh vegetables, then dive into their special wheat bread. All the while I'm saving room for the lavish main course: delicious steak, mouth-watering chicken, or savory fish—whatever I want. It is a delight for the senses.

By the time we finish, our stomachs are full of healthy food and completely satisfied. I lean back in my chair and bask in the contentment. In that moment, my friend usually urges, "Don't stop now...you gotta have our deluxe brownie dessert." Within minutes, Ashley and I find ourselves attempting to stuff down luscious bites of warm chocolate. But we are so full that we can rarely finish it. So we have the chocolate boxed up to take home and share together. The whole dining experience is marvelous—especially when the waiter bids us farewell without leaving a bill.

In many ways, I consider eating at my friend's restaurant a picture of experiencing Christ's passion for you and me. As the Son of God, Jesus has the authority to freely bestow God's riches on whoever receives His invitation. He knows that our hearts are starving for love, and He desires to nourish us with His unconditional acceptance. Song of Solomon 2:4 paints a picture of this truth: "He has brought me to his banquet hall, and his banner over me is love."

Just as your stomach has a constant need for healthy food, your heart has a constant longing for true love. To meet this craving, Jesus offers you an unending supply of His love. It's like eating free meals for the rest of your life at an amazing restaurant. The forgiveness, approval, and life of Christ act as the soup, appetizer, and entrée to satisfy your hunger. He furnishes everything to meet the yearnings within you—all you have to do is receive it.

Once Jesus fulfills your heart with His nourishing love, you are in the position to share romance with another person, which is like eating a chocolate dessert after a nutritious meal. At my friend's restaurant, Ashley and I filled ourselves with healthy food first. Once our stomachs were fully nourished, we enjoyed eating a large fudge brownie. In contrast, if all we ever ate was chocolate, our health would deteriorate.

Likewise, as Christ's love becomes your primary source of nourishment, you place yourself in the best position to enjoy dating and marriage. Rather than romance ruining your life, it offers the opportunity for His abundant love to overflow through you to another person. Romance can benefit you only when you do not depend upon it for survival. Therefore, as a Christian single, you can enjoy dating relationships responsibly because they aren't necessary for your fulfillment in life. Moreover, if you never marry, you are no less valuable or complete because you are already married to Christ.

God never intended dating and marriage relationships to be the focus of your life. Instead, God established human romance to illustrate your intimate union with Jesus. When you single out someone who specifically attracts you and sacrificially love that person, you taste the passion that Christ feels for you.

No one in this world loves you more than Jesus does. He is the only Person who promises to cherish, celebrate, and live His life within you for all eternity. If you have never experienced the pure passion of Christ, I invite you to do so today. In your heart, receive Him as your loving Husband.

*D*early beloved, we are gathered here today to celebrate this joyous occasion. Two people have come together with a specific attraction for one another and the desire to be formally united in marriage. Being assured that no legal, moral, or religious barrier hinders their union, they will now join hands and answer the following questions:

> Do You, Jesus Christ, take the reader of this book to be Your lawfully wedded wife? Do You promise, in the presence of God and these witnesses, to unconditionally accept, sacrificially love, and forever be faithful to this reader?

> I do.

> Do you, reader, take Jesus Christ to be your lawfully wedded Husband? Will you take Him as the sacrifice for your sin? Will you love, honor, and worship Him? Do you promise, in the presence of God and these witnesses, to forsake loving other people in your own strength and allow Jesus Christ to faithfully love them through you for as long as you live?

> I do.

By the authority I have as the Minister of the gospel and the Creator of the universe, I now pronounce you Husband and wife. What I have joined together, no man can separate.

Friend, I hope that this book has unveiled how the love of Christ can transform not only your dating relationships but also your entire life. As the bride of Jesus, you no longer need to impress, control, or manipulate people to quench your heart's desire for love. Jesus has freed you from the pressure of finding human affection, so you can delight in the pleasure of His complete approval.

I pray that you will always regard your spiritual marriage as your primary source of love and view earthly romance as the chocolate dessert. May Jesus Christ inspire and invigorate your dating relationships. Above all, may you experience the power of His pure passion throughout your life.

Passion awaits you....

NOTES

Chapter 1—The Power of Pure Passion

1. *Webster's New World Dictionary,* s.v. "Passion."
2. *The New Testament Greek Lexicon,* s.v. "Toy." www.biblestudytools.net.

Chapter 2—Passion from Heaven

1. Mike Mason, *The Mystery of Marriage* (Sisters, OR: Multnomah Books, 1985), p. 47.
2. *Webster's New World Dictionary,* s.v. "Acceptance" and "Approve."
3. Steve McVey, *Grace Walk* (Eugene, OR: Harvest House, 1995), p. 73.
4. Bob George, *Growing in Grace* (Eugene, OR: Harvest House, 1991), p. 63.

Chapter 3—Where's the Passion?

1. Malcolm Smith, *No Longer a Victim* (Tulsa, OK: Pillar Book and Publishing Co.), pp. 34–35.
2. Ibid., p. 37.
3. "Session 4: Journey to the Cross," *The Grace Life Conference Workbook* (Association of Exchanged Life Ministries, 1998), pp. 26-29.

Chapter 4—Choose Your Passion

1. Henry Cloud and John Townsend, *Safe People* (Grand Rapids, MI: Zondervan Publishing House, 1995), p. 20.
2. Ibid.

3. Ibid., p. 21.

4. Neil Clark Warren, *Finding the Love of Your Life* (Colorado Springs, CO: Focus on the Family Publishing, 1992), pp. 53-56.

Chapter 5—The Pursuit of Passion

1. Joyce Cohen, "On the Net, Love Really Is Blind," *New York Times*, January 18, 2001. www.nytimes.com/2001/01/18/technology/18date.html.

Chapter 6—The Enemy of Passion

1. Bill Gillham, *What God Wishes Christians Knew About Christianity* (Eugene, OR: Harvest House, 1998), p. 105.

2. "Session 2: The Nature of The Flesh," *The Grace Life Conference Workbook* (Association of Exchanged Life Ministries, 1998) p. 7.

3. Dan Stone and Greg Smith, *The Rest of the Gospel* (Richardson, TX: One Press, 1999) pp. 197-200.

Chapter 7—The Bond of Passion

1. "Joins" is a translation of the Greek word *kallo,* which means "to glue, to glue together, cement, fasten together, to join or fasten firmly together, to join one's self to, or to cleave to." The New Testament Greek Lexicon. www.biblestudytools.net.

Chapter 10—The Sabotage of Passion

1. Bill Gillham, *What God Wishes Christians Knew About Christianity* (Eugene, OR: Harvest House, 1998), p. 261.

2. Ibid., pp. 260-61.

3. Neil Clark Warren, *Finding the Love of Your Life* (Colorado Springs, CO: Focus on the Family Publishing, 1992), p. 75.

4. Ibid., pp. 74-75.

About the Author

Rob Eagar knows the heartache and frustration that many singles encounter. In his twenties, Rob experienced intense rejection and disappointment when he was suddenly abandoned by his wife. Yet his pain was transformed into joy when he discovered his true identity in Jesus Christ. Since then, Rob has shared the passionate love of Christ with thousands of singles, young adults, and college students across America.

Rob holds a bachelor's degree in marketing from Auburn University and a doctorate in Dating from the School of Hard Knocks. He started teaching singles in 1994 and has spoken at churches including Willow Creek Community Church, Saddleback Church, and McLean Bible Church. His message has been featured nationwide on the CBS Early Show and CNN Radio, and in Christian Single Magazine. Rob resides in Atlanta, Georgia with his wife, Ashley, where they attend North Point Community Church.

When Rob isn't speaking or writing, he enjoys hiking, tennis, and playing his drums as loud as possible. However, Ashley prefers that he join her to quietly paint, work in their garden, or watch Jane Austen movies.

For more information about Rob Eagar or to request him for a speaking engagement, please visit www.Rob Eagar.com

Other Good
Harvest House Reading

FINDING YOUR PERFECT MATE
H. Norman Wright

In this helpful book, Norm offers words of wisdom, encouragement, and guidance on one of life's most important decisions. Along with scriptural insights, he contributes valuable insights based on his years as a premarital counselor.

SINGLE, SASSY, AND SATISFIED
Michelle McKinney Hammond

With her humorous, tell-it-like-it-is style, Michelle combines scriptural principles for daily living with inspirational stories, quotes, and experiences of life, love, and men. If you're a single woman, you will embrace and celebrate your singleness.

SECRETS OF AN IRRESISTIBLE WOMAN
Michelle McKinney Hammond

You will discover the rules and scriptural principles about love that ensure solid, godly relationships. Secrets offers practical advice, inspiring prayers, and study questions to help you understand and recognize real love.

WHAT TO DO UNTIL LOVE FINDS YOU
Michelle McKinney Hammond

Drawing from 16 years of being single and counseling single women, Michelle offers women practical, godly advice on how to handle sexual temptations regardless of past experience, develop internal and external beauty, and wait joyfully for God's timing.

HARVEST HOUSE
PUBLISHERS